General World and Jewish History	Century Beginning	50 Jewish Messiahs
Black Death devastates Europe (1348) Spanish pogroms against Jews (1391)	1300	...51)
First printed books (1450) Turks take Constantinople (1453) Spanish Inquisition begins (1481) Jews expelled from Spain (1492) Columbus sails to America (1492) Jews expelled from Portugal (1497)	1400	Messiah of Beyreu (1495)
Ines, the Maid of Herrera (1500) Maria Gomez of Chillon (1500) Protestant Reformation begins (1517) Sack of Rome (1527) Henry VIII divorces, establishes Church of England (1532)	1500	Asher Lemlein (1500) David Reuveni (1523) Shlomo Molkho (1525) Isaac Luria (1534–72) Hayim Vital (1542–1620) Ludovico Diaz, Messiah of Setubal (1540)
Dona Juana Enriquez (1600) Ines Pereira (1600) Manasseh ben Israel (1604–1657) Antonio de Montezinos finds Lost Tribes in South America (1644) Oliver Cromwell (r. 1653–1658) Shabbatai converts to Islam (1666)	1600	Shabbatai Zevi (1626–1676) Nehemiah Kohen confronts Shabbatai (1666) Suleiman Jamal (d.1666) Abraham Miguel Cardozo (1626–1706) Mordechai ben Hayyimof Eisenstadt (c.1630–1706) Yehuda Leib Prossnitz (1670–1730) Yehoshua Heshel Tzoref (1633–c.1700) Hayim ben Shlomo (c.1655–1716) Nehemiah Hiyya Hayyun (1650–1726) Jacob Filosoff Querido (c.1650–1690)
Jacob Frank converts to Christianity (1759) Declaration of Independence (1776)	1700	Baruchya Russo (d. 1720) Berechiah Filosoff (d. 1740) Moshe Hayim Luzzatto (1707–1747) Jacob Frank (1726-1791) Eva Frank becomes "The Lady" (1790–1817) Ba'al Shem Tov (1700-1760) Nachman of Bratslov (1772–1811)
Disraeli publishes *The Wondrous Tale of Alroy* (1833) American Civil War (1861–1865)	1800	Israel of Ruzhin (1797–1850) Itzak Eizik of Komarno (1806–1874) Shukr ben Salim Kuhayl ("Shukr Kuhayl I") (c. 1821–1865) Shukr Kuhayl II (appeared 1867) Yusuf Abdallah (1895)
Donmeh expelled from Salonika (1924) WWII (1939–1945) and the Holocaust State of Israel established (1948) Beta Israel "Lost Tribe" returns to Israel (1984, 1990)	1900	Menachem Mendel Schneerson (1902-1994)

50
JEWISH
MESSIAHS

50 JEWISH MESSIAHS

Jerry Rabow

The untold life stories of 50 Jewish Messiahs since Jesus
and how they changed the Jewish, Christian and Muslim worlds

gefen גפן
publishing house בית הוצאה לאור
JERUSALEM ◆ NEW YORK

Typesetting and Cover Design: S. Kim Glassman • Jerusalem, Israel

1   3   5   7   9   8   6   4   2

Gefen Publishing House
POB 36004, Jerusalem 91360, Israel
972-2-538-0247 • orders@gefenpublishing.com

Gefen Books
12 New St., Hewlett, NY 11557, USA
516-295-2805 • gefenbooks@cs.com

www.israelbooks.com

Printed in Israel

Send for our free catalogue

ISBN 965-229-288-5 (alk. paper)

Library of Congress Cataloging-in-Publication Data:
Rabow, Jerry, 1937-
50 Jewish Messiahs: the untold life stories of 50 Jewish messiahs since Jesus and how
they changed the Jewish, Christian and Muslim worlds / Jerry Rabow. p. cm.
1. Jewish messianic movements—History. 2. Messiah—Judaism.
I. Title: Fifty Jewish Messiahs. II. Title.
BM615.R33 2002 • 296.3'36—dc21 • CIP Number 2002021093

For my parents, Belle and Milton Rabow,
who taught me the love of words

and

For my wife, Lola,
who taught me the words of love.

I believe with complete faith in the coming of the Messiah
—Traditional Jewish prayer, *Ani Ma'amim*

CONTENTS

PREFACE

THE FIRST rule of writing is often said to be "Write what you know." This book breaks that rule. Unlike the experience of most non-fiction writers, I was as surprised by what this book had to say as most of its readers will be. Even after becoming familiar with the stories told here I was left with many important questions.

First, how could there have been fifty or more Jewish Messiahs, but I had never heard of most of them? A few of the Messiahs were, admittedly, relatively minor local figures. Many others surely deserve knowing. They were significant historical persons during their time. They often generated broad international impact, engaged in substantial dealings with important world church or government figures, and inflicted major consequences on the Jewish community.

Like many contemporary American Jews, I have read secular and Jewish history books, attended Jewish lectures, taken Judaism courses as a child and as an adult, and heard Jewish sermons. Despite this, all I knew about Jewish Messiahs was that there had been someone named Shabbatai Zevi and a Jacob Frank after him, and they were both despicable characters. I had heard of some of the other characters in this book only in their roles as scholars, philosophers, or military heroes, but without hint of their messianic aspects.

So how could someone like me have remained oblivious to the names and lives of fifty Jewish Messiahs? The answer, I believe, is communal shame. For two thousand years Jews have reacted with deep shame to the disappointment and pain of the outcomes of their Messiah episodes. In some instances this reaction was formally institutionalized, as when the rabbis ordered destruction of community records regarding Shabbatai Zevi. In other situations the followers themselves kept documentation secret and often tried to destroy papers when the movement finally ended, as with the Donmeh and the Frankists. In many cases Jewish writers who would normally chronicle the history of something as important as a Messiah movement perhaps felt that it did not represent the Jews' finest hour. Most rabbis and teachers in the modern era have been understandably reluctant to initiate public discussion about incidents that could make Jews appear gullible or foolish.

The resulting relative absence of historical materials and cumulative analysis generated some difficulties for this book. True, I was not attempting a scholarly, definitive history of the Jewish Messiahs. I simply wanted to reveal their stories. Even this limited goal presented real challenges. The sources that record these stories are often highly unreliable. For any particular story there may be several conflicting versions, which in many cases may be retellings of the same underlying source. Because the stories in this book span two thousand years, many of the earlier stories have little claim to historical reliability. The early stories frequently present only a compilation of travelers' anecdotes, folk tales, and religious polemics, either from fervent believers or from equally fervent Jewish skeptics or non-Jewish anti-Semites. Nevertheless, even where unreliable, many of these older stories deserve retelling because they were believed by and exerted great influence over generations of Jews and non-Jews.

I have tried not to make up anything (even if that would have made a good story better), but I often had to choose among conflicting details and alternative versions from different sources. My choices have been determined primarily by my desire to tell the stories in the versions that have been an active part of Jewish and world history. I have noted some places where modern scholarship now speaks with a very different voice. My choices also have been restricted primarily to those sources that are available in English.

But it isn't only the "What" of history that is uncertain in these stories. The other basic "W"s of history—Who, When, and Where—are similarly uncertain. The names of most people and places discussed in this book were originally in Hebrew or other local languages. There is no universally recognized system of transliteration from Hebrew to English. Consequently, different reference works often use different spellings for the same name. Again, I have had to choose and did so primarily based upon what appeared to be the most popular and easily pronounced English spelling.

Dates are complicated by the fact that the Jewish calendar follows a lunar year that starts sometime in September or October of the solar calendar year. These Jewish lunar years are not numbered from the date of Jesus' birth, of course, but from a biblical calculation of Creation, traditionally figured as 3,760 years earlier. Therefore, when a story containing a Jewish calendar date was first translated from Hebrew, early retellings may have dated the occurrence in one of the two overlapping secular calendar years falling in that Jewish calendar year. As a result, many of the dates given in this book could be off by a year due to translation. Other dates may be only approximate (even where not so indicated) because of uncertainty or conflict within the historical record.

As for locations, cities have often changed their names, and national boundaries have shifted. For the convenience of the reader I have sometimes used modern names of nations, cities, or population groups even though they did not yet formally exist at the time of the described events.

This book contains several features designed to help the reader with many of these issues. To provide a guide to historical placement, I have included a timeline showing the dates for each of the Messiahs mentioned in the book, together with markers for significant historical events providing context to the stories. Foreign or technical terms are briefly defined when first used in the text, but the Definitions section also includes an expanded glossary for ready reference as the terms are encountered later in the text.

In addition, although this book is not presented as a formal academic work, I have included in the Appendix some notes offering interested readers expanded treatment of some collateral events or connections related to the main stories.

The most important challenge, perhaps, was selecting which aspects of history the book should address. This was a very personal decision for me. I started researching these stories because of my surprise that such an important area of my religious and historical heritage could have remained unknown to me until now. As I began to uncover the stories, my focus shifted away from the basic facts or even the theological implications of the Jewish Messiah stories. Instead, I became fascinated with the role of the Jewish Messiah movements in general history, what these stories told of the personalities of the Jewish Messiahs and their believers, and the interaction and impact the stories had in the world of their time. Others have written, and I hope will continue to write, about the many important issues not directly addressed by this book: when and why messianic movements arise, what factors determine the extent of a Messiah's acceptance, how we should judge the Messiahs of the past, how we should react to future Messiahs, and what role messianism plays in modern Judaism.

This book chooses to examine humanity, not divinity. This is history, not theology. I hope you will agree that these stories of the Jewish Messiahs present a significant and intriguing mosaic (if not quite Mosaic) portrait of the universal human need for optimism and hope, and the range of triumphs and tragedies that can flow from this. Along the way, we can share some wonderful stories.

ACKNOWLEDGMENTS

MOST NON-FICTION books owe much to the research and writings of previous authors and teachers. This book owes everything. Because this is a compilation of stories, it is entirely dependent upon the previous tellers and re-tellers of these tales. I want to express my gratitude to the authors of my sources for providing the histories and analyses that I have followed. I have not only learned the stories from them but have also been instructed and influenced by their approaches and theories. A discussion of principal sources appears after the text.

Beyond this acknowledgement of specific literary sources, I also want to express my deep appreciation for the many teachers of Jewish theology, history, philosophy, Torah, and Talmud who have created and nurtured my interest in Judaism, and especially my rabbis, Rabbi Harold M. Schulweis and Rabbi Edward Feinstein of Valley Beth Shalom Synagogue, Encino, California, and my other principal recent teachers, Rabbi Jerry Danzig, Rabbi Ben-Zion Bergman, Professor Arnold Band, and Sarah Har-Shalom, my current guide to the Hebrew Bible. Living in Los Angeles, I was fortunate to have access to the fine library resources of the University of Judaism, the University of California at Los Angeles, the Los Angeles Public Library, and Valley Beth Shalom Synagogue, as well as a splendid variety of classes and lectures through the University of Judaism Department of Continuing Education, the UCLA Center for Jewish Studies, and Valley Beth Shalom Synagogue.

I am pleased to be able to fulfil my promise to Susan Golant, a generous and helpful instructor in the UCLA Writer's Program, to offer public thanks for her instruction and advice.

My friends and family expressed such enthusiastic support and unbounded confidence for this project that I could never have disappointed them with anything short of publication. Among those who were especially generous in sending me current articles, reading and commenting on preliminary drafts, or helping with the logistics of getting published were Rabbi Harold M. Schulweis, Sheila Alperstein, Rhoda Barnhard, Bob Barnhard, M.D., Jeanie and Ron Blanc, Drs. Tema and Steven Galaif, Marvin Shapiro, and my children, Victoria Rabow, Ph.D., and Russ Hirsch, Barbara Bowman and Michael Rabow, M.D., and Amy Rabow Johnson and Grant Johnson. Barbara and Michael's critical insights and efforts were particularly important in convincing me that I needn't try to write everything that I thought I knew about the topic.

My hours at the computer were lightened by many sweet visits from my older grandchildren, Maddy and Cole. I was even able to delight in their curiosity about the keyboard and mouse once I learned to "save" as soon as they started to climb into my lap.

I am deeply indebted to the authors who generously agreed to review the manuscript and offer personal reactions to the book as a whole: Rabbi Harold Schulweis and Rachel Naomi Remen, M.D. Jeff Herman was a friend as well as an enthusiastic and loyal agent. Bob Bleiweiss's generosity of time and talent was crucial to the final version of this book and its publication. My every dealing with Ilan Greenfield and his staff at Gefen Publishing House was positive and helpful.

Of course, the person who contributed—and suffered—most with this book is my wife, Lola. She lovingly and cheerfully put up with so much: sitting through my telling the same stories to friends and acquaintances innumerable times; waiting for household tasks and repairs that I could never see being quite as important as just finishing the next sentence, paragraph, or chapter; and generally enduring my being busy researching and writing more than any husband should be busy doing any one thing. I started out thinking that this book was my gift to myself; in a very real sense, this book is Lola's gift to me.

Jerry Rabow

Introduction
The Jewish Concept of Messiah

A N EXCELLENT formula for instant dispute, if not riot, is to try to talk about *the* Jewish concept of anything. The absolutely best thing about Judaism—or the absolutely worst thing, depending upon a particular Jew's theological affiliation—is that there is no single expression of official dogma defining Jewish belief. You may wonder how Jews could be universally agreed since the Middle Ages as to the precise wording of the Bible, while they still struggle among themselves today with major theological disagreements about Judaism's core beliefs. The answer is *interpretation*.

While Jews agree on exactly what the Bible says, two millennia of interpretation have led to divergent—even incompatible—beliefs as to what the Bible means. Judaism has no infallible central ecclesiastic authority able to promulgate rules binding upon all Jews. The first great work of basic Jewish interpretation of the law, the Talmud (completed in the fifth to seventh centuries) is not in the form of a proclamation, but rather a sort of transcript of centuries of interpretational debates among generations of rabbis.[1] Along with the theological disputes that it records, the Talmud also interweaves myths, stories, and playful, fanciful explorations of Jewish history and religion.

Just as the Bible was not the last word, neither was the Talmud. Subsequent rabbinic commentaries through the centuries, continuing to today, further inform—and sometimes inflame—the general discussion.

Thus, it is not surprising that there is no single, authorized, official Jewish view of the Messiah. The best we can do is to note some central themes and prominent variations of the traditional Jewish concept of Messiah.

   While the origins of the Messiah idea can be traced to several
early apocryphal writings, the popular Jewish concept of Messiah
generally begins with the biblical verses of several of the
Prophets, particularly Isaiah and Zechariah. These Jewish
prophets pictured the messianic era simply as a time of universal
peace, when the exiled Jews would be returned to their Holy Land
as a sovereign people—an event often called the "Redemption,"
"Return," or "Restoration." The Jews would then reassume their
membership (or perhaps preeminence) among the world's nations.
This idyllic messianic era would be ushered in by the appearance
of the Messiah, who would be a descendant of King David.

   These initial expressions do not describe the Messiah as a
supernatural miracle worker, or even as someone whose special
efforts are needed to bring on the messianic era. The initial Jewish
Messiah idea referred simply to the temporal Jewish leader who
will reign when the messianic era arrives. The very word
"Messiah" (in Hebrew, Moshiach, meaning "anointed") does not
imply any miraculous or divine powers, but merely refers to a
priest, king, or prophet who undergoes the formal ritual of
anointment with oil to enter upon his role.

   Jewish theology is ultimately shaped by the communal
experiences of Jews. As the Diaspora experience became
increasingly marked with suffering, despair, and death, Jews
needed more, and the Messiah concept was elaborated. To keep
hope alive during desperate times, Jews began to emphasize the
version of the Messiah myth predicting that the arrival of the
messianic era would be preceded by the infliction on the world of
terrible "birth pangs" (a term used by Isaiah). Under this view, the
Messiah would come only after the very lowest point of history,
marked by international chaos and destruction and, in particular,
great suffering for the Jews.[2]   Thus, the worse their current
circumstances became, the more reason Jews had for believing
that the Messiah not only would come, but would come soon.

Because of the seemingly unbridgeable contrast between the miserable reality of the Jews' lives and their sweet dreams of universal peace, it was natural for Jews to believe that it would take a miracle worker to bring on the change. In this manner, the Jewish Messiah figure was transformed from an ordinary leader to a man of miracles—from a king who would preside over the new era to a military hero whose divinely invincible powers would win the final battle.

Of course, one difficulty with a requirement that the Messiah must be a divine, miraculous being is what to do when the Messiah is not ultimately successful. What can you say when the miracles were not enough? With lots of practice Jews developed several answers. First, not everyone agreed that the Messiah would be a miracle worker. Moses Maimonides (1135–1204) was one of Judaism's greatest philosophers, commentators, and theological authorities of any era. Although he wrote extensively about the Messiah, Maimonides was an intellectual rationalist who strove to bring Judaic beliefs into harmony with Aristotelian "scientific" truth. Thus, his concept of the Messiah returned to the original biblical view: the Messiah would be an ordinary but enlightened leader who would reign at the time of the messianic era. Until the messianic era arrived, it was obvious to Maimonides that all purported Messiahs must fail.

Maimonides' somewhat cool rationalizing of the messianic dream was not enough for the burning needs of a desperate people. A second doctrine that developed to answer the issue of the failed Messiah declared that God provides a Messiah for each generation, but none of those Messiahs would be permitted to usher in the messianic era unless the righteousness of the Jews of that generation merited it.

Perhaps borrowing a page from Christian doctrine, followers of a particular Jewish Messiah often dealt with the apparent failure and death of their hero by denying that the ordinary processes of failure and death applied in his case. Their Messiah had not failed; his job was only temporarily incomplete. Their Messiah had not died; he somehow escaped death and was in hiding, or his soul survived the execution of his body and would return, perhaps in the form of a successor Messiah. Even if he had indeed died, he would surely be resurrected to complete the messianic transformation.

Finally, the failed Messiahs of Jewish history gave rise to a remarkable variation of the basic Messiah myth: Not one, but two Messiahs will bring on the End of Days. First, a tragic Messiah, the Messiah of the House of Joseph (through Joseph's son, Ephraim), will appear. This military figure will begin the battle to retake Jerusalem, but will die in the war at the hands of the military chief of the evil forces, King Armilus. Although slain, this Messiah will be resurrected upon the arrival of the Messiah of the House of David. The appearance of the second, triumphant Messiah will unite all the peoples of the world and begin the era of messianic peace.[3]

The Jewish Messiah doctrine is really a collection of multiple, often inconsistent doctrines: Either the Messiah will be an ordinary leader, or the Messiah will be a divine miracle worker. Either there will be only one Messiah, or there will be one in each generation throughout history. Either the Messiah must be successful, or the defeat and death of a failed Messiah must first precede the triumph of the ultimate Messiah. Either the Messiah will not die, or he can die but will be resurrected. Either the people can hasten the coming of the Messiah through their acts of piety, or the messianic age will come when it will come.[4]

The Bible and subsequent Jewish history are filled with Jewish heroes, many of them charismatic and popular civil, military, or religious leaders who played great roles in the story of Judaism. In the face of the great theological diversity in the Jewish Messiah concept, how can we decide which historical figures should be regarded as Jewish Messiahs?

For many general examinations of the Messiah phenomenon,

and in particular for this book, a good working definition would be to treat as Jewish Messiahs *those Jews who had a significant impact on history because of their express claims to be the leader chosen by God to bring on the messianic era, or because their Jewish followers believed they were such a Messiah.*

This definition intentionally ignores the question of whether a particular Messiah figure was sincere or a fraud, sane or deluded, or beneficial or injurious to his followers and to the Jewish people at large. The sincerity of a Messiah claimant often is not easy to judge from the record. The impact on history of some patently fraudulent Messiah figures often exceeded the consequences of other, apparently sincere, claimants. The terms "false Messiah" or "failed Messiah" are not helpful.[5] We need only look out our windows at the world today to see that all the Jewish Messiahs have as yet been false or failed Messiahs.

These Messiahs of the past two thousand years are unquestionably a part of Jewish heritage, but does the Messiah remain a contemporary Jewish concept? Because the Messiah idea became the core of Christian theology, it no longer feels much like a comfortable Jewish concept for many liberal Jews. Although belief in the Messiah remains an indisputable principle of Orthodox Jewry, much of the rest of contemporary Judaism no longer focuses on the Messiah with the traditional intensity.

On this point, it is instructive that most of the Jewish Messiah figures of the past two thousand years arose before the "modernization" of Judaism that began with the eighteenth century European Enlightenment movement. After thousands of years of Jewish exile, powerlessness, and suffering, the dawning of the modern scientific age brought to Jews the promise of full citizenship in the nations of Europe where they lived. This prize came at a price. A messianic myth that still promised the Jewish people ultimate sovereignty would suggest dual loyalty. If Jews were to be accepted as loyal citizens of France or Germany, they could not cling to an idea that they were also a separate nation, and that their Messiah would ultimately restore them to a superior national status in the world. Modern liberal Judaism therefore gave up the Jewish national aspect of the Messiah myth.

The traditional Jewish Messiah's ability to work miracles presented a similar problem. When liberal Jews felt uncomfortable clinging to the expectation of a supernatural miracle-worker while claiming membership in the modern, scientific world, they gave up the miraculous aspect of the Messiah myth.

Despite these theological modifications made only in these last few hundred years, the traditional Messiah idea has been a basic, crucial element of faith for most of the Jews living in most of these past two thousand years, including many Jews today. This book does not advocate either increasing or restricting the role of the Messiah concept in contemporary Judaism. This book tells the Messiah stories simply because Jews have a right to know about their messianic heritage, and non-Jews likewise are entitled to have access to what is, in many ways, their shared history.

Finally, what about Jesus? He and his contemporary followers were Jewish. Both he and his followers believed that he was the Messiah. They told stories about the miracles he performed. His followers became members of another religion, and subsequent generations have awaited his return to begin the messianic era. But all of this could likewise be said about Shabbatai Zevi, the most powerful Jewish Messiah since Jesus. Shouldn't a book of stories of the Jewish Messiahs include Jesus?

The question of Jesus, like so many other Messiah questions, was addressed by Maimonides. It was politically unfortunate, perhaps, that he made his comments in the context of explaining how to distinguish between failed Messiahs (who nevertheless may be "wholehearted and worthy") and the true Messiah. In his *Mishne Torah,* Maimonides proposed a very simple test: if a learned and observant Jew, descended from David, unifies the people of Israel and leads them in the battles for the Holy Land, then he can be treated provisionally as a possible Messiah. But if he dies without ushering in the messianic era by rebuilding the Temple and gathering all the Jews, then we know that he was not the true Messiah. Maimonides closed this analysis by noting that such a standard, if applied to Jesus, would require the conclusion that Jesus was not the true Messiah. This last point was so inflammatory that Christian censors would not permit it to be included in the published work. Even today, the previously censored provisions are typically printed as a footnote to the standard version of Maimonides' book.

I believe that under the definition used to select the fifty names in this book, Jesus does indeed qualify as a Jewish Messiah. I have nevertheless limited these stories to the Jewish Messiahs appearing after Jesus because this book is not the appropriate source for readers to learn about Jesus. Fine historical and theological scholarship about Jesus abounds. His followers flourish. His story has been and continues to be told. I felt that the stories of the other, forgotten Jewish Messiahs (over fifty of them since Jesus) are the ones that this book should tell.

Chapter 1

THE FIRST JEWISH MESSIAH

Apparently Bar Kokhba himself never directly claimed to be the Messiah. The title he used on the coins and documents of his new state was "Nasi" (prince) of Israel. He was not descended from King David. How, then, did Simeon Bar Kokhba become the first Jewish Messiah?

ALTHOUGH THE first Jewish Messiah after Jesus remains well known among Jews today, he is not generally remembered as a Messiah.[6] Today Jews celebrate Simeon Bar Kokhba (ca. 100–135 CE) only in his more famous role as an outstanding Jewish general and civil ruler. This selective recollection is not due to any inaccessibility of historical materials. Although Bar Kokhba lived two thousand years ago, we have the benefit of substantial historical and archeological materials describing his activities. Unlike the situation for so many of the early Messiahs, we can tell a fairly fully documented story for this first Messiah. In addition to a colorful Talmud debate among the rabbis, we have letters and governmental decrees written by Bar

Kokhba, coins struck during his reign, and imperial Roman documents.

Extreme circumstances first called forth this great Jewish general and statesman. In the beginning of the second century, Rome was committed to both military subjugation and at least partial cultural assimilation of a vast part of the world. During the reign of Emperor Trajan, surprisingly strong Jewish armed resistance arose in North Africa (Libya and Egypt), Cyprus, Mesopotamia (Iraq), and Judea (Palestine). The uprisings were overcome, but only through the use of massive Roman military force brutally punishing or exterminating much of the Jewish populations. When Trajan died in 117 CE, his nephew Hadrian succeeded him as Emperor of Rome.

Seeking to improve upon his uncle's bloody and costly policies, Hadrian tried a new approach to pacify the Judean population and avoid further Jewish revolt. Suddenly Hadrian became champion of the Jewish cause. The Emperor began by executing Quietus, the hated general who had been used by Trajan to subdue Judea. Then, with great fanfare, Hadrian began a project that irresistibly signaled to the Jews the approach of the messianic era—Hadrian undertook the rebuilding of the Jewish Temple in Jerusalem, at the location where Titus had destroyed the Second Temple in 70 CE. It is said that, in order to ensure absolute fidelity to the biblical requirements for the construction, Hadrian placed the project under the direction of Onkelos, a renowned biblical translator and commentator (and famous convert to Judaism). It is difficult even to imagine what the course of Jewish history might have been if Hadrian had gone through with his plans to build the Third Temple for the Jews.

Instead, the Emperor stopped the project because of the concerns of his generals and the Church. They warned him that if he reestablished the Jews in their Temple in Jerusalem, the Jews would become too powerful. In place of the messianic dreams that Hadrian's initial plan had stirred up, his reversal sparked bitter resentment in the Jews. The emperor's new policy unleashed a vicious spiral of reciprocal hostility. Hadrian's daughter was killed, and he blamed the Jews. He punished them with an ever-increasing list of anti-Jewish laws, including barring Jews from entering their beloved city of Jerusalem. He renamed the city Aelia Capitolina in honor of himself and the god Jupiter. His final step was announcing his decision to convert the aborted Jewish Temple project to the construction in its place of a pagan temple of Jupiter.

This was the challenge that summoned young Bar Kokhba from the countryside to lead the Jewish resistance. With a combination of shrewd generalship, charismatic leadership, and detailed administration of his organization, Bar Kokhba managed repeatedly to defeat the best of the Roman armies. The Jews took almost a thousand cities and villages, and built and occupied fifty fortresses. They even briefly retook the city of Jerusalem and drove out its Roman governor. The Jewish army continued to grow, as fanatically dedicated followers joined the victorious Bar Kokhba.

The Romans, on the other hand, were forced to call in their legions from many distant parts of their empire to try to stop the revolt. Finally, desperate to reverse the Jewish victories, Hadrian turned to Julius Severus, the Roman general who had subdued a similarly fierce native opposition in Britain. Even this great general, with the resources of the entire empire, had to realize his inevitable victory by a slow and costly war of attrition. The Romans besieged, starved out, and retook the villages and fortresses one at a time, until the final siege of Bar Kokhba's army at the city of Betar (a few miles southwest of Jerusalem). The bloody war potentially threatened the entire empire. Rome's cumulative military losses were so great that Emperor Hadrian began his war report to the Roman Senate without the customary line, "I and my army are well."

During this time, Bar Kokhba not only held off the military

might of Rome, but also managed to establish a new civil government of Israel, which he ruled for three years. He administered title to land and enforced stringent procurement demands to feed and support the army. He even issued coinage for the new government, overstamping Roman coins and redating them as being issued in the first or second year of "Jewish independence."

Bar Kokhba was an effective but harsh administrator. His communications with his officers often threatened punishments if his demands were not faithfully performed. Several of his letters indicate that he and his army were following Jewish ritual practices even during those war years. He sought delivery of the "four species" of plants used for celebration of the holiday of Succoth, and was concerned that fruits delivered to his army had been properly tithed (setting aside a portion for religious contribution). He and his army apparently wore traditional prayer shawls (*talesim*), honored the Sabbath restrictions on activity, and observed the rules prohibiting the mixture of plant or animal species (*shatnes*).

Bar Kokhba's secret weapon was the fanatic loyalty of his army. Initially his soldiers were required to demonstrate their devotion by cutting off the tip of a finger. When the rabbis complained about this practice, Bar Kokhba substituted a test whereby new recruits had to uproot a cedar tree. It is reported that 200,000 men qualified under the first test, and an equal number under the second.

All of this shows no more than a popular and effective general and head of state. Apparently Bar Kokhba himself never directly claimed to be the Messiah. The title he used on the coins and documents of his new state was "Nasi" (prince) of Israel. He was not descended from King David. How, then, did Simeon Bar Kokhba become the first Jewish Messiah?

His story features only a few of the typical signs of Messiah status. While his phenomenally successful military campaign against the might of Rome seemed miraculous in the colloquial sense, his success was attributed not to magic but to his military skills and the fierce loyalty of his troops. At most, the personal stories about Bar Kokhba emphasize his unusual strength—during sieges, he is said to have caught incoming Roman catapult stones and tossed them back—but his legend lacks true miracle stories.

Some argue today that Bar Kokhba did take active steps suggesting his claim to Messiah status. He seems to have imposed some ritual requirements that satisfied the more stringent teachings of the school of Rabbi Shammai, rather than the generally accepted standards of the school of Rabbi Hillel. Rabbinic legend has it that the rulings of Shammai will be substituted for those of Hillel only when the Messiah comes.

Basically, Bar Kokhba became the Messiah because of the people's strong need for a Messiah in that unique historical era. The Jews' yearning for the Restoration had not been so strong and specific since the destruction of the Second Temple over eighty–five years earlier. After their messianic hopes had been inflamed by the plans of the Emperor Hadrian to rebuild the Temple, the resulting deep disappointment created a demand for the appearance of the Messiah to fulfil Hadrian's promise.[7] The people expected a Messiah, and prince/general Bar Kokhba was the obvious candidate.

Although most rabbis of that time opposed the concept that Bar Kokhba, with his undistinguished background, could be the holy Messiah, popular belief in him received crucial support from Rabbi Akiba, one of the most revered teachers and sages of the time, and himself a man of the common people.[8] Akiba transformed Bar Kokhba from ordinary farmer to the first Jewish Messiah by a simple stroke: Akiba changed the man's name. Bar Kokhba himself apparently used the family name Bar Kosevah, or Bar Kosiba. It was Akiba who renamed him "Bar Kokhba," meaning "son of the star," a biblical term alluding to the Messiah.

Unfortunately, poetical allusion can be a two-edged sword. Some of the other rabbis, who did not share Akiba's belief that the Messiah had arrived, delighted in referring to Bar Kokhba as "Bar Koziba," which means "son of lies." (Then, as now, rabbinic discourse was not always maintained at the highest intellectual level.)

The famous Akiba's proclamation that Bar Kokhba was the King Messiah was simply not sufficient to win over the rest of the rabbis. The depth of their skepticism is evident from the stern rejoinder by Rabbi Yochanan ben Torta recorded in the Jerusalem Talmud: "Akiba, grass will sooner grow on your chin before the Messiah comes."[9]

According to the rabbis, even when Bar Kokhba was leading Israel's army in its victories over Rome he was doing it in the wrong manner. Despite his observance of Jewish religious ritual in his personal life, Bar Kokhba relied solely on his military efforts to achieve his victories rather than recognizing the ultimate role of God in the outcome. The rabbis were particularly enraged when they heard that before his battles Bar Kokhba didn't pray for God's help, but only asked that God would remain neutral and permit the Jewish army to win by force of arms. Instead of acknowledging dependence upon the divine, Bar Kokhba would pray: "Master of the world, neither help nor embarrass us."

If most of the rabbis scoffed at the messianic title for Bar Kokhba when he was vanquishing the Romans and establishing an independent Jewish state, their opposition naturally intensified when the victories were reversed. Over a half million Jews died from military action as the Roman army gradually recaptured the Jewish strongholds, and many more died from starvation and disease caused by the Roman sieges. Rabbi Akiba himself was captured and martyred by the Romans. The entire Jewish opposition finally shrank until there was nothing left except the grim resistance to the Roman siege of the sole remaining Jewish stronghold—the city of Betar.

The stories about the end of that resistance and the end of this first Jewish Messiah tell much about Bar Kokhba and how he was viewed. The basic story is that the Romans finally succeeded only through colossal trickery. A Samaritan entered Betar and contrived to be observed whispering to Rabbi Eleazar, Bar Kokhba's uncle and the spiritual head of the besieged city. When confronted, the Samaritan falsely confessed that he had been conspiring with Rabbi Eleazar to give up the city to the Romans. At this revelation, an enraged Bar Kokhba is said to have kicked his uncle Eleazar to death.

At this point, even Bar Kokhba's messianic supporters in Betar must have developed doubts about their Messiah King. The rabbis decided to use a scientific test in order to resolve the question of whether Bar Kokhba was the Messiah. According to Jewish legend, the Messiah will be a man of such perfect judgment that he will be able to judge without relying upon the possibly misleading evidences of either sight or sound. This must mean, the rabbis concluded, that the Messiah should be able to judge a man by smell alone. Therefore, they demanded that the blindfolded Bar Kokhba determine by smell the guilt or innocence of an accused man. Bar Kokhba failed history's first "smell test."

Whatever the truth of this story of Bar Kokhba's test, apparently the rabbis of Betar did have Bar Kokhba killed after he executed Rabbi Eleazar. Without Bar Kokhba, the Jewish resistance crumbled. The Romans brutally overran Betar, killing all that they could find of the Jewish men, women and children.

Bar Kokhba's reign as the first Jewish Messiah ended with universal condemnation from the rabbis for the terrible loss of lives, the destruction, and the punitive Roman laws caused by the rebellion. They attributed Bar Kokhba's downfall to his personal shortcomings of arrogance and cruelty. Subsequent Jewish history has somewhat softened the judgment of Bar Kokhba.

First, Bar Kokhba's story may have inspired popular acceptance of the two-Messiah theory. Jews decided that it was first the destiny of a warrior Messiah of the House of Joseph to fail and fall in battle before a subsequent Messiah of the House of David could appear and achieve ultimate success. Under this theory, even the calamity of a Bar Kokhba could be seen to advance the coming of the messianic era.

Secondly, the tragedy of Betar is said to have occurred in the 9th day of the Hebrew month of Av, the day also ascribed to the destruction of the First and Second Temples. Thus, when the 9th of Av is observed by Jews today as a solemn fast day of national mourning, they remember Betar more as a calamity attributable to God's inscrutable will, rather than as a failure for which the first Jewish Messiah should be blamed.[10]

Chapter 2

THE SECOND MOSES

Moses of Crete appeared and... claimed that he was a prophet sent by God to return the Jews to Jerusalem.

SINCE ITS inception, the Jewish State in Israel has had a special connection with the island of Crete. Crete is the probable origin of the Philistines, the archenemies of the first Jewish kingdom under Saul and David. Ultimately it was the land where the British interred Jewish refugees attempting to settle in Palestine after World War II just before the establishment of the modern State of Israel. In the midst of this great span of history, the second Jewish Messiah appeared in fifth-century Crete.

The Roman Empire had split between East and West in 395. Subsequently, Byzantine Emperor Theodosius II (401-450) imposed harsh laws of oppression on the substantial Jewish community of Crete. Both these events—the breakdown of general world government and the discrimination suffered by the Jews—seemed to be the "birth pangs" signaling the beginning of the messianic process.

The times were also especially ripe for the appearance of a Jewish Messiah because of some rabbinic calculations. The Talmud predicted that the Messiah would appear during the 85th Jubilee (fifty-year period) since the creation of the world. This would fall in the years 4200-4250 in the Jewish calendar, corresponding to the years 440-490. Another popular Jewish prediction held that the exile of the Jews from the Holy Land that began with the destruction of the Temple would not last longer than the original period of enslavement in Egypt. This calculation placed an outside date for the new Redemption at no later than 468. There was even a general non-Jewish prophecy that the era of Rome would exist for 1,200 years, a period that would expire in 447.

All of these calculations, predictions, and conditions pointed to the mid-fifth century for the beginning of the messianic era. Certainly, the suffering Jewish community of Crete was ready. All they lacked was a Messiah. So God sent Moses.

At least, that's what the man claimed. In 440, Moses of Crete appeared and began a year of traveling throughout the island and preaching to the Jews. He claimed that he was a prophet sent by God to return the Jews to Jerusalem. As befits both the name that he picked and the absence of available alternative transport, this second Moses promised to take the Jews to the land of Israel in the same manner as the first Moses did. He would simply cause the Mediterranean Sea to split, and the Jews would walk from Crete to Jerusalem on dry land.

Moses of Crete developed a large and enthusiastic following. The Jews ignored their business affairs, gave their wealth (which wouldn't be needed in the messianic era, after all) to their Messiah, and assembled on a cliff overlooking the sea on the day he had fixed for the miracle.

There is a well known Talmudic gloss on the original parting of the Red Sea by the first Moses, relating that Moses didn't actually part the waters and lead the Israelites across. Rather, one man plunged into the water and doggedly continued until the water reached his nostrils; only after this demonstration of faith did God part the waters for the Jews. Whether influenced by this story or perhaps by either simple prudence or outright chicanery, Moses of Crete likewise did not try to part the waters first. Instead, he ordered his followers to trust him and jump into the sea. He stayed behind on the cliff, with their money.

The believers did jump, and many were drowned. Puzzled Cretan fishermen rescued others. It is reported that most of the survivors converted to Christianity. Moses of Crete disappeared along with the wealth of his former followers.

Chapter 3

THE SYRIAN MESSIAHS
THE UNKNOWN MILITANT AND THE INFAMOUS MIRACLE WORKER

Serenus vowed vengeance on the Jewish community, and then came up with a most inventive way to carry out his oath. He became a Messiah.

THE NEXT Messiah account that has come down to us is so sketchy that we don't even know the name of the Messiah—only that he existed. He is called simply "The Syrian Messiah," and his story is a brief one: In about 643, a Jew from Bet Aramaye, Syria, announced that he was the Messiah. He convinced a small group of about four hundred men to follow him into military revolt. The local government's army swiftly overcame the insurgents, killed all the men and their families, and crucified the Syrian Messiah.

If nothing else, the Syrian Messiah established a pattern that would be followed later by several minor Jewish Messiahs. He proclaimed himself to be the Messiah, he led a small group of believers in a brief military rebellion against the local authorities, and the exercise ended with the death of the Messiah and his followers.

The next Jewish Messiah in Syria did not follow the simple model of his nameless predecessor. The next Messiah had many names, together with a style that was much closer to Moses of Crete.

Indeed, there was little typical about Serenus, also called Serene, Severus, Saria, Saur, and Zonoria, who appeared at about 720. His collection of names may simply have been based upon "Serene," a corruption of "Syrian," so if the title hadn't already been taken by his predecessor, Serenus too might be known as "The Syrian Messiah."

Serenus was originally a Syrian Christian who had converted to Judaism. Apparently his career as a divine Messiah had a rather earthy origin. He was discovered after he had seduced a Jewish girl in Sumaria. Stung by the public rebuke, Serenus vowed vengeance on the Jewish community, and then came up with a most inventive way to carry out his oath. He became a Messiah.

Preaching around the city of Mardin in Syria (Kurdistan), Serenus claimed to be the Messiah, or his prophet, and quickly developed a strong following. His popularity seems to have been closely tied to developments in the Muslim world in which he and his followers lived. First, there had been the remarkable series of Muslim victories over the Christian successors to the Roman Empire, which peaked a few years before Serenus with the Muslim siege of Constantinople, the capitol of the Byzantine Empire, in 718. These Muslim victories certainly satisfied the Jewish belief that the Messiah would appear after a period of world chaos and upset of established governments.

Second, the Muslim authorities had begun to relax their restrictions on the autonomy of the Jewish communities in their lands. A wealthier and more educated Jewish community therefore gained greater direct access to the teachings of the Bible. The result was an anti-Talmudic, anti-rabbinic trend in the religious thought of the Jews.

Serenus was able to capitalize on this explosive combination of high messianic expectation and anti-rabbinic sentiment. Since the Jewish Messiah myth said that Talmudic rules of Judaism would not be applicable in the messianic era, Serenus abolished many rabbinic laws, such as fixed prayer services, observance of the second day of holidays, the rabbinic elaboration of the laws of kashrut (kosher foods), ritual purity laws regarding contact with dead bodies, and the rules concerning marriage contracts. (Given his recent difficulties with the Jewish maiden in Sumaria, this last law change must have given him special satisfaction.)[11]

The most enticing part of his program occurred when Serenus announced that he was ready to begin the messianic era immediately. He promised that he would miraculously fly the Jews back to the Land of Israel. The Jews of Syria believed him. Word of their acceptance, in turn, reached Jewish communities in Spain and France, infecting them with similar enthusiasm. This was a trip no one wanted to miss.

Spanish and French Jews came to Syria ready to give over to Serenus their wealth and possessions (soon not to be needed in the messianic era). Muslim religious tolerance was one thing, but this group of foreign Jews giving away their wealth was too much for the Arab authorities to ignore. The government seized the property of Serenus's local and foreign followers, and arrested the Messiah himself.

The record displays typical conflict as to what happened next. Some say that Serenus admitted to the Caliph Yezid that he was not sincere, but was intentionally misleading the Jews. Under this version, the Caliph was so incensed by such base trickery that Serenus was turned over to the Jewish community authorities for punishment, and was killed. By another account, it was the Emir Ambiza who captured Serenus, and who decided to impose a pragmatic test of the Messiah's authenticity by having him executed. When no miracle saved Serenus, his Messiah status was finally disproved, at least to the Emir's satisfaction.

In any event Serenus died, and his movement ended with him. His former followers petitioned Babylonian rabbinic authorities for readmission to the ranks of traditional, normative Judaism without the need to undergo formal rituals of re-conversion. This was granted (except for those who had disregarded laws of family purity) on condition that the repentant followers make public penance and declare their loyalty to the rabbinic laws of the Talmud.

Chapter 4

THE PERSIAN MESSIAH DYNASTY

Although he taught that he was the final and most developed in a line of God's holy prophets, Abu Isa preached a uniquely ecumenical message for a Jewish leader of that time, especially for a Jewish Messiah.

JEWISH MESSIAHS are generally expected to work miracles, but probably the most impressive miracle of the Messiah Abu Isa, in the mid-eighth century, was the man himself. As a Messiah, Abu Isa founded the first significant Jewish sect since Temple times, reinterpreted standards of ritual observance, established a minor dynasty of successor Messiahs, and led a huge revolt that threatened to overthrow the Muslim government of Persia. The miracle was that the man who accomplished all this, Abu Isa, started out as an uneducated tailor named Yitzhak ben Yakov.

He first appeared near Isfahan, Persia (Iran), around 750, claiming that he was the last of the great prophets and was about to bring on the messianic age. Abu Isa declared that God had appeared to him and told him that he would be greater than all of the preceding holy prophets. Abu Isa primarily described himself as being a prophet or messenger of the Messiah, but his followers believed that he was indeed the Messiah. Because he was not descended from the Davidic line, Abu Isa may have considered himself as only the Messiah of the House of Joseph, destined to lead the Jews in a military battle for freedom.

Before he became a great military leader this uneducated artisan somehow managed to write books and statements announcing his claims and promulgating new religious doctrines. Many times in history, the role of the Jewish Messiah has included decreeing changes in Jewish ritual practice. Some Messiahs (such as Serenus) abrogate rabbinic or even biblical laws because such rules are supposed to become unnecessary in the messianic era. Others go in the opposite direction, adding to traditional rules and demanding an even higher level of personal piety and observance from their followers, because only an observant people will deserve to see the messianic era. Abu Isa was one of these latter Messiahs. His religious rules imposed very strict ascetic standards of holiness, including prohibiting eating meat or drinking liquor, abolishing divorce, and increasing the standard three daily prayer services to seven a day.

Thus, besides displaying many of the markers of a traditional Jewish Messiah, Abu Isa's story seems to borrow elements from the Christian and Muslim Messiah stories. Like Jesus, Abu Isa demanded greater personal piety from his followers. (The name "Isa" may have been derived from the Arabic name for Jesus.) Like Mohammed, Abu Isa was able to write books setting forth his religious doctrines despite his illiteracy, or at least lack of education. Abu Isa's followers took this authorship as a miracle confirming that he was the Messiah.

Although he taught that he was the final and most developed in a line of God's holy prophets, Abu Isa preached a uniquely ecumenical message for a Jewish leader of that time, especially for a Jewish Messiah. He not only declared that both Jesus and Mohammed were authentic prophets for their followers, but he urged his own followers to read the Gospels and the Koran for the wisdom they contain.

In addition to Abu Isa's ability to write his books, his followers cited other miracles showing that he was God's Messiah. In fulfillment of one theme of the Jewish Messiah myth, it was said that Abu Isa had traveled beyond the legendary Sambatyon River and made contact with the Ten Lost Tribes of Israel, who were believed to be living there awaiting the messianic era. As another miracle, his followers reported that, when Abu Isa led them into battle, he would draw a line on the ground encircling his men, and the enemy could not harm them. He would then ride to the Muslim army and single-handedly defeat them. Whatever the actual method of his military victories, Abu Isa was very successful. His popularity continued to grow, and he developed a large army ready to follow him into battle—perhaps as many as ten thousand followers in all.

The beginning of Abu Isa's downfall is told by Maimonides four hundred years later in his *Letter to Yemen* (1192). In seeking to caution twelfth century Yemenite rabbis against tolerating the popular belief in a new local Messiah, Maimonides tells that, as Abu Isa's army marched beyond Persia and approached Baghdad, the Sultan sent out a group of local rabbis to determine if Abu Isa was truly the Messiah. It is not surprising that according to Maimonides—Judaism's greatest intellectual—the Baghdad rabbis concluded that an uneducated tailor could not be the Messiah. The rabbis interrogated Abu Isa's followers and concluded that he had not performed any miracles that would verify his claims. They persuaded his followers to stop the revolt, and the Sultan even gave money to the followers to convince them to leave his country. Maimonides points out that after the invasion threat ended, the Sultan recovered his money by fining and punishing the Jews of Baghdad. Thus, the adventure ended, as essentially all Jewish Messiah appearances in history have ended, very unhappily for the Jews.

The death of the Messiah Abu Isa followed in 755. He joined his forces with Abu Sinbad's revolt against the Abassid government. When the revolt failed, Abu Isa was captured and killed near the city of Rhagae (present-day Rae, Iran). His followers refused to accept the fact of his death. They insisted that he had somehow escaped, that he had fled to a cave in the local mountains, and that he would surely reappear when the time for the messianic era finally arrived. So strong was this belief that his followers established a sect of Judaism (known variously as the Isavites, Issuniyim, Issunians, Issiyim, or Isaphanites) that eventually moved to Damascus, and continued for almost 300 years after the death of Abu Isa. Because the Isavites did not weaken the ritual rules but followed an even more stringent version of traditional Jewish law, the rabbis considered the sect as fully within Judaism.

In addition to his sect of believers, Abu Isa also left behind him a short chain of successor Messiahs. In about 800, a pupil of Abu Isa rose to prominence. Yudghan (Yehuda) of Hamadan was called "the Shepherd." This was a fitting name, for, unlike the warrior Abu Isa, Yudghan did not believe in fighting. He preached an extension to Abu Isa's teachings, not only continuing the practices of fasting and abstinence, but also developing a sophisticated, anti-rabbinic theology emphasizing individual free will, abolishing Sabbath and holiday observance, and recognizing two levels (explicit and esoteric) of Torah interpretation. Although Yudghan only proclaimed himself a prophet, his followers, the Yudghanites, declared him to be the Messiah.

While the Yudghanite movement did not last as long as the Isavites, it did continue for a century or so after Yudghan's death. His death itself proved noteworthy among most Jewish Messiahs—Yudghan died a natural death.

Yudghan's movement had substantially diminished importance compared to Abu Isa's. The third and last member of this Persian dynasty of Messiahs continued this slide to obscurity. Yudghan's pupil and successor was Mushka, a ninth century messianic figure who returned to the military style of Abu Isa. He led his Mushkhanites in several battles. The Persian Messiah dynasty closed on a note of insignificance when Mushka fell in his final battle at Qum, leading a troop of only nineteen soldiers.

Chapter 5

THE MESSIAH ACCORDING TO MAIMONIDES

How could Maimonides, this man of logic and science, become the rabbinic authority most involved with the Jewish Messiah myth?

IT SEEMS exceedingly strange today to learn that the rabbinic name most closely associated with the Jewish belief in Messiah and with the history of Jewish Messiahs up to his time was Moses Maimonides (Rabbi Moses Ben Maimon, 1135–1204). After all, we generally regard Maimonides as the greatest Jewish rationalist philosopher of his or any other era. He earned fame as a physician as well as a rabbinic scholar, and his philosophy pursued the rigorous logic of Aristotle. How could Maimonides, this man of logic and science, become the rabbinic authority most involved with the Jewish Messiah myth?

The answer lies in the curious alignment of circumstances in Maimonides' life. As a young boy, he and his family fled from anti-Semitic persecution by a militant Muslim sect that gained control of Cordoba, Spain. Settling in Egypt, Maimonides succeeded his father as a leading physician, becoming personal physician to the Caliph of Egypt. Because of his great intellect he became the chief rabbinic authority of his time, writing authoritative answers (responsa) to religious questions sent to him by Jewish communities throughout the world. He also wrote monumental and definitive works organizing, summarizing, interpreting, and making accessible to rabbis and lay Jewry alike the entire corpus of biblical and Talmudic law.

Maimonides resolved the apparent conflict between his love of Torah Judaism and his love of Aristotelian philosophy by reinterpreting Judaism to conform to his rationalist, scientific view of the world. He believed that Judaism is a matter of divinely revealed truths, but that logic and science are also true. Maimonides harmonized the inconsistencies between biblical revelation and scientific integrity by treating problematic biblical descriptions as allegory and poetry rather than literal truth. In this process he generally strove to rationalize and clarify traditional elements of Jewish belief rather than eliminate them.

Perhaps this is why Maimonides not only refused to discard messianic belief from Jewish theology, but he actually elevated the rabbinic and folk doctrine of Messiah to a core belief of Judaism. Jews then, as now, wanted to know just which of the many items of belief and tradition were absolutely necessary to constitute authentic Judaism. Maimonides answered with a list of thirteen beliefs he deemed essential to true Judaism. His "Thirteen Principles" are still recited by Jews today in the poetic form of a popular prayer (the Yigdal). The twelfth of Maimonides' fundamental principles of Judaism requires belief in the Messiah.

Jews reject Freud's observation that man creates the concept of God and endows Him with the qualities man needs. Still, it is difficult to ignore how conveniently Maimonides' version of the Messiah mirrors his own abilities and passions for intellectualism, rationalism, and study. Maimonides agrees that Jews must believe that the Messiah will come. Beyond that point, however, Maimonides rejects much of the popular beliefs about the Messiah and the messianic era.

To begin with, by the time of Maimonides many rabbis had spent great efforts scanning the Bible in order to calculate and predict when the Messiah would appear. Most of these calculations, perhaps expressing their authors' personal longing for the messianic era, happened to place the expected Coming at or just a few years after the time of making the prediction. Maimonides prohibited messianic predictions because they only served to whip up the people's gullibility and vulnerability to fraud.[12]

According to Maimonides, we will know when the Messiah arrives because he will usher in a messianic era marked by dramatic changes instantly apparent to all. Traditional Jewish belief emphasized that the Messiah would be known by his ability to perform miracles, but Maimonides described a very different Messiah. Maimonides' Messiah would not be a supernatural, super-human miracle worker. Indeed, the efforts of the Messiah would not even be directly responsible for bringing on the messianic era. Maimonides' conception of the Messiah was an ordinary man, although wise and inspiring, descended from the House of David, who would be the popular ruler of the Jews when the messianic era began. Miracles would not cause the messianic era to occur. Instead, the Messiah's reign of peace would simply be the marker and enabling circumstance of the beginning of the messianic age.

In Maimonides' view, the messianic era would not merely be a general paradise on earth; it would be a very particular paradise— one that Maimonides himself surely would enjoy and one that he believed everyone should enjoy. In a word, it would be an era of *study*. Maimonides saw the messianic era as a logical progression: The wise governance of the Messiah-King would inspire worldwide peace. Without war and strife, man could be productive and earn his living with only a little effort and time. The ease of such a life without stress would result in people being healthier and living longer (although they would not live forever). Then all that extra time of leisure and extended life would be devoted to study, which in turn would lead to increased social cooperation and scientific advances. Once achieved, these benefits would then form the foundation for repeated new cycles of messianic improvements in the condition of life on earth.

Here was an image of the messianic era that was fit for a Maimonides, as well as for the entire people of Israel as he dreamed they would become. Since reality often falls short of dreams, Maimonides still had to deal with the reality of the twelfth century.

Chapter 6

MAIMONIDES' MESSIAHS

The Messiah volunteered, "Chop off my head and I shall revive at once!" ... So they chopped off his head.

GIVEN MAIMONIDES' elevated ideal of the messianic era, we can understand his distress when, at the close of the twelfth century, he was asked about a Jewish Messiah who appeared in the Yemenite community. Rabbi Jacob ben Nathanel al-Fayyumi of Yemen wrote to Maimonides asking what should be done about a growing popular belief in an unnamed local Messiah. Regardless how difficult such a question might ordinarily be, it was obvious to Maimonides that this particular claimant could not possibly be the Messiah—the man was a fool.

Maimonides' response, his *Letter to Yemen* (1192), is a treasure of the histories of then-recent Messiahs, Jewish messianic traditions, Maimonides' own views of the Messiah in Judaism, and his stinging judgment of the Yemenites' belief in their current Messiah.

Maimonides cites the histories of four previous Messiah claimants and the problems they caused the Jewish communities that listened to them. He starts with the story (previously recounted in Chapter 4) of Abu Isa in Persia in the eighth century. In relating this story, Maimonides cites the Sultan's resulting punishment of the Baghdad Jewish community as evidence for the conclusion that Jewish enthusiasm for claimed Messiahs generally ends badly for the community.

The second Messiah described in the *Letter to Yemen* is the "Lyons Messiah," who appeared at about 1060. Originally assumed to be in Lyons, France, this incident probably occurred in Leon, Spain.[13] Wherever it took place, the story presents a typical local messianic phenomenon of a miracle-worker who quickly developed a following, and almost as quickly suffered swift and crushing military action from a concerned government. The miracle performed by the Lyons Messiah was that he could fly (an extremely useful skill for someone whose role would include somehow transporting the Jews from their Exile to the Promised Land). He demonstrated his powers on moonlit nights by climbing tall trees and soaring like a bird from treetop to treetop. In reaction to his growing popularity, government forces raided the Jewish quarter, killing the Messiah and many of his followers.

At least the Lyons Messiah volunteered for the job. The third Messiah described by Maimonides was only a reluctant draftee, but he was punished all the same. This Messiah incident happened in Cordoba, Spain (Maimonides' birthplace), at about 1100. Maimonides relates the story as told to him by his father. The beginning of the twelfth century was a time ripe for the appearance of the Messiah. It may have appeared then that the world chaos and Jewish suffering predicted to precede the Messiah had indeed begun with the advent of the First Crusade (1096). In addition, in Muslim-controlled Cordoba, Jews were probably concerned with the Muslim threat that they would lose their status as a protected people (*dhimmi*) under Islam if the Jewish Messiah did not appear within five hundred years after the appearance of Mohammed.

This period was calculated, under the lunar calendar, to expire in 1107. The result was the next Jewish Messiah.

The reign of this reluctant, silent Messiah began when some local Jewish astrologers announced that they had seen signs in the heavens indicating that the Messiah had already appeared, and that he could be found in Cordoba. Since no one had been making messianic claims or performing miracles, the best this group could do was to search the local Jewish community and pick the most virtuous, pious, and educated man available as the likely candidate. They settled upon a young teacher named Ibn Ayre. Ibn Ayre never expressed enthusiasm for his new role. He apparently never made any claims to be the Messiah or performed any miracles. Even without his encouragement, he became the center for a growing group of followers who themselves performed predictions and miracles that they attributed to his influence.

Probably to preempt reaction by the Muslim authorities, the leaders of the Jewish community took action. They brought Ibn Ayre to the synagogue and declared that, while he had not actively made messianic claims, his very silence had encouraged his followers to continue in their folly, creating danger to the community. He was found guilty of failing to instruct his followers that they were acting in error and in violation of Jewish beliefs. For his silence in the face of the beliefs of his followers, Ibn Ayre was publicly flogged, fined, and excommunicated. The Jewish community similarly punished his major followers.

The fourth Messiah story told by Maimonides in his *Letter to Yemen* describes the history of Moshe (Moses) al-Dar'l, who appeared 1120. Again the time was ripe for a Messiah in Muslim territory, because when the five hundred year period from the time of Mohammed had been recalculated from lunar to solar years, the expiration date for Jews' protected status under Islam moved from 1107 to 1122 (five hundred years from the journey to Medina).

Moshe al-Dar'l came to Fez (Morocco) after studying in

Muslim Spain. He soon attracted notice by making a series of successful public predictions. When his bizarre prediction that it would rain blood came true (the region suffered some sort of reddish precipitation) his followers were convinced. Although he didn't claim to be the Messiah, the people probably believed he was, and they were certain that he could at least predict when the Messiah would come. The people got what they hoped for.

Moshe al-Dar'l had a dream and announced that the Messiah would appear on the evening of the next Passover. This was certainly an appropriate date for a prophet named Moses to predict for the second Exodus. At the urging of the confident Moshe al-Dar'l, his followers prepared for the messianic era by selling their property and by borrowing as much as they could from the Muslims—at ten-to-one interest. These steps gave the followers immediate benefits of wealth, and would cost nothing, since once the Messiah appeared, the Jews would not need property and would not have to repay debts.

Unfortunately this proved to be overly aggressive financial planning. When Passover came but the Messiah didn't, the Jews of Fez were ruined. In a sense, one element of the prediction did come true—at least one Jew was transported to the Promised Land. That one Jew was Moshe al-Dar'l himself, who had to flee for his life from the irate Muslim creditors. Before he fled, he made several more miscellaneous predictions, as a sort of farewell gift to the Jewish community. Strangely, it is reported that these last predictions also came true. Thus, his gift of prophesy apparently failed him only once, but that was enough to transform Moshe al-Dar'l from a miraculous prophet into one of the tragic Jewish Messiah figures of history.

Maimonides' history of recent Messiahs completed, his *Letter to Yemen* could then turn to the current problem he had been asked about: What should the Yemenite rabbis do about the new Jewish Messiah?

Since Maimonides saw the messianic age as an era of study and
knowledge, it was obvious to him that the claimant who was so
popular in Yemen at the end of the twelfth century was not the
Messiah. The Messiah will be a proud, wise leader, greater than
Moses. The Yemenite claimant, however, was merely meek, which
is not a characteristic of the Messiah. Moreover, the Yemenite
claimant was clearly not wise, but ignorant. He preached that
people should give all their wealth to the poor. To Maimonides, this
is illogical stupidity, not charity. If people give everything to the
poor, then the recipients would become rich and the donors would
become poor, so that the money would just have to be given back,
ad infinitum. Maimonides explains that it is to avoid just this
foolishness that the Talmud restricts permissible charitable giving
to 20% of one's wealth.

If the Yemenite claimant is foolish, he cannot be the Messiah.
What, then, should the rabbis do? Maimonides' *Letter to Yemen* is
clear in his judgment of the participants. The claimant himself
sounds sincere but insane, and so cannot be blamed for believing
he is the Messiah. The ordinary Jews of Yemen who believed in
this Messiah were generally uneducated and ignorant, so they
cannot be blamed for their belief. Maimonides reserves all blame
for the rabbis and educated leaders of the Jewish community, who
should have understood the lessons of history and taken the
appropriate steps to stop this Messiah.

And how do community leaders stop a Messiah? Since the
claimant is mad, Maimonides advises the leaders to put him in
chains in order to protect the community against scorn and
persecution from the Muslim authorities. Apparently, this advice
was not acted upon. Maimonides incidentally reports the outcome
in another letter, written two years later (1194) to the Jews of
Marseilles. About a year after Maimonides had cautioned against
just such a consequence, the local Muslim ruler captured the
Yemenite Messiah and demanded a miracle that would confirm

that he was a true Messiah. The Messiah's response at least confirmed Maimonides' opinion of him.

The Messiah volunteered, "Chop off my head and I shall revive at once!" His captor was duly impressed, and acknowledged that such a miracle would not only prove that the man was the Messiah, but would also establish to the whole world that Judaism was the true faith and Islam was false. So they chopped off his head.

Chapter 7

THE JEWISH MESSIAH FROM THE ARABIAN NIGHTS

Alroy was quickly able to develop a substantial following when he declared that he was the Messiah and had been sent by God to complete the work that his father had begun—to lead the Jews to retake the land of Israel.

THE STORY of the Messiah David Alroy (active c.1120–1147) reads like something out of the *Arabian Nights*, but with a decidedly Jewish flavor and a rather unique ending. After all, Jewish Messiahs throughout history have died in various ways. A few died in their beds, while many were beheaded. Only one Messiah managed to do both.

David Alroy was born as Menahem ben Shlomo al-Duji, in the city of Amadia, Kurdistan, in the early twelfth century. The subsequent choice of the name David was obviously a claim to the Davidic lineage that was generally considered a requirement for the Messiah. Unlike most Jewish Messiahs, Alroy did not grow up a stranger to messianism. It was a family enterprise.

Alroy's father, Solomon ben Duji, had worked together with Palestinian scribe Ephraim ben Azariah ibn Sahalun to found a movement to return the Jews to the Promised Land. Solomon and Ephraim operated in Khazaria, in central Asia. Everything about David Alroy's life story seems exotic, and this connection with the land of the Khazars was no exception.

Khazaria was an important nation ruling an area of the Caucasus and the Crimea adjacent to the Black Sea. Around 740, King Bulan of Khazaria is said to have taken a very unusual action: he summoned Christian, Muslim, and Jewish leaders to debate the question of which was the true religion. Unlike the later forced, sham "disputations" of the Spanish Inquisition, this debate was genuine. The debate also differed from the Inquisition disputations in another important way—the Jews won.

The prize was unique. As a result of the debate, the King, his court, and a substantial portion of the entire nation of Khazaria converted to Judaism. The nation continued as a Jewish state for several hundred years. Then, in a manner unusual even for an area of traditional political instability, the nation and people of Khazaria simply disappeared after a military defeat in 965, leaving essentially no surviving cultural heritage, political aftermath, or physical artifacts. That a single nation could undergo these two rare events—national conversion to Judaism and ultimate disappearance almost without a trace—seems so bizarre that it is difficult to accept this as the documented, historical reality it is, rather than a mere myth.[14]

In Khazaria, Alroy's father, Solomon, claimed to be Elijah, the prophet whose traditional role it is to precede the coming of the Messiah. As the prophet of the Coming, Solomon then declared that the Messiah was, in fact, his son David. David Alroy not only enjoyed this unique family heritage, but also possessed other personal advantages for his role as Messiah. He was intelligent, educated, handsome, and charismatic. He even received an ideal education for a Messiah, studying under the Gaon (academy head) of Baghdad, where he excelled in both Jewish and secular studies. His science studies included a subject that would become most helpful to this Jew from the *Arabian Nights*—Alroy learned magic.

The Jews of the region were ready for the Messiah to appear. They were caught in the middle of the Christian-Muslim conflict, and had suffered from both Crusader attacks and local Arab government massacres. It did not take much imagination for the Kurdistan and Persian Jews to see that their lives fulfilled the prediction for miserable times before the Messiah's appearance.

Alroy was quickly able to develop a substantial following when he declared that he was the Messiah and had been sent by God to complete the work that his father had begun—to lead the Jews to retake the land of Israel. He aimed to accomplish this through a military campaign, although he also imposed on his followers a pious regimen of fasting and prayer to become worthy of the Return.

His fame and popularity surged with a story of his miraculous escape from prison: Captured and imprisoned by the Sultan of Persia, Alroy declared that he would reappear before the monarch in three days. As he promised, three days later he magically walked through the iron gates of his cell and appeared before the Sultan. The palace guards were mysteriously paralyzed from being able to move against Alroy, who fled. The army pursued him to the banks of the Gozan River, where Alroy made another, even more dramatic, escape. Alroy is said to have eluded capture by taking the kerchief from around his neck, spreading it on the water, and floating across the river on it. Lacking the Messiah's magic, the army had to continue the pursuit the old-fashioned way. They obtained boats and searched the riverbanks, but found no one. Alroy had fled (some said he had magically transported himself) to the city of Amadia, Kurdistan, his birthplace and base of support.

The city controlled an important Crusader trade route, and was also the home of a revolutionary Muslim movement that was willing to support Alroy against both the Christians and the local Muslim government. Alroy sent word to his followers in the immediate area and the surrounding regions of Azerbaijan, Persia, and Mosul (now in Iraq) that the battle to return to Jerusalem was about to begin. He had his followers smuggle weapons into Amadia by concealing them in their clothing, and the resulting armed force was able to capture the city briefly.

Political reality set in before the Messiah could fulfil the dream of gathering the Jews and leading them back to the Promised Land. The Sultan of Persia threatened to kill all of the Jews in the country unless Alroy were stopped. In response, the leaders of the Jewish community declared that Alroy was not the Messiah, and forbade the people from following him. Since even authoritative decrees are not much of a match for magic and miracles, it is not clear whether the Jewish community leaders would have been able to end Alroy's power by simple fiat. The solution came from a neighboring Turkish ruler, Sultan Zun al-Din, a friend of the Jews, who saw that only the death of Alroy would save the Jews from Persian reprisals.

According to the most popular version of the story, Zun al-Din gave Alroy's father-in-law ten thousand gold pieces to kill him. The father-in-law accomplished this by getting Alroy drunk one night and cutting off his head while he was sleeping in bed. The Messiah's head was sent to the Sultan of Persia, but this failed to satisfy him. The Sultan still wanted to imprison and punish Alroy's followers, and the Jews had to purchase their peace and liberty by a community payment of one hundred talents of gold.

It is difficult to escape the sense of the oriental exotic when one pictures David Alroy in perhaps his greatest moment, a calm smile on his face, sitting cross-legged on a small square of kerchief, floating across the Gozan River, leaving the soldiers of the Sultan on the bank shaking their fists in impotence and frustration.

Alroy deserves to be called the "Jewish Messiah from the *Arabian Nights*" for more than just his exotic and magical legend. Like the heroes of the *Arabian Nights,* Alroy became a significant figure in world culture, and not merely a local folk hero, because his story was immortalized in writing. In his case it took two famous authors to preserve and spread the legend.

Most of what we know about Alroy comes originally from the account of a traveler and diarist who happened to be in the region immediately after the events. When Benjamin of Tudela published his *Book of Travels* (*Sefer ha-Massa'ot*), he gave the world a "historical" (but uncritically accepting) account of the Messiah Alroy. Tudela's book was translated and republished over the years, and a 1784 version eventually came into the hands of one of the important new nineteenth century English novelists. One can speculate about what it was in the story of a twelfth century Jewish Messiah that so captured the interest of this young author, who would soon have to struggle against his own Jewish heritage in order to become the great Victorian Prime Minister of England. Whatever the causes, in 1833, Benjamin Disraeli published his historical novel, *The Wondrous Tale of Alroy,* which further fictionalized, transformed, and expanded Alroy's legend.

The story of David Alroy did not survive only in the pages of literature. As has often happened with charismatic Messiah figures, some of Alroy's followers would not accept his death as the end of his story. His followers in Azerbaijan continued to believe that he had somehow escaped by miracle once again, or that he would in any event return to complete his mission. The sect that they founded, the Menahemites, continued their belief in him, and regularly invoked his name to bind their oaths. David Alroy managed to remain a popular folk hero for more than eight hundred years. References to his miracles can still be found in the folklore of contemporary Israel's Kurdistan immigrants.

The strangest postscript to the story of David Alroy was

embodied in the shameful, fraudulent exploitation of his legend perpetrated in Baghdad around the time of his death. The reaction of the Jews of Baghdad to reports of David Alroy's miracles was perhaps predictable from a prior event in about 1120 (around the time when Alroy first made his appearance). A fragment of a document found in the Cairo Geniza (a sacred burial place for discarded documents that contain God's name) tells the earlier story.

The daughter of Joseph, a Baghdad physician, had a vision in which Elijah appeared to her and announced that the Redemption was about to begin. The Jewish community was elated by the prospect of the Messiah's approach. Since earthly governments were about to end forever, the Jews defied their civil rulers. They refused to wear their required badges of identification, and even stopped paying their taxes. This last step obviously was never contemplated as part of the limited freedom of religion allowed to the Jews by Muslim law, and the Caliph of Baghdad reacted promptly. He threw the leaders of the Jewish community into prison.

Before they could be punished, Elijah reappeared. This time, Elijah made his appearance to the Caliph himself, in a dream. Apparently chastened by his personal encounter with the ghost of the Jewish prophet, the Caliph ended the incident by releasing the Jewish leaders upon payment by the community of the standard ransom.

Far from discouraging the Baghdad Jews from believing later reports of a new Messiah, this incident apparently only raised the community's messianic expectations, making the time ripe for the infamous postscript to the story of David Alroy. The report of the impact of the David Alroy story on the Baghdad Jews is based upon anti-Jewish sources, so it is possible that the resulting portrait is highly distorted.

According to the report, when news of David Alroy's miracles (but probably not yet of his death) reached Baghdad, two Jewish crooks took advantage of the community's excitement. The men forged a letter from Alroy promising to transport the Jews of Baghdad to Jerusalem on a particular night. As has been promised by various Messiahs through the centuries, Alroy was to fly the Jews to the Promised Land on the wings of angels.

The Jews of Baghdad believed the forgery, made new clothes for the trip, and worried about the practical logistics of the miracle. They debated how families would be able to find one another when they landed in Jerusalem, and whether the trip would take so long that nursing infants should travel in their mothers' arms rather than with their own angels. The believing Jews gave their money to the two crooks, and on the appointed night, the Jewish community went up to their rooftops.

The people sat there until dawn. By morning, their dreams of Redemption were gone, along with their money and the two confidence men. This event not only made the Jews an object of derision in the Muslim community, but according to one report, even the Jews of that generation would date subsequent family births and events as being so many years after "the Year of Flying."

Chapter 8

THE MESSIAH WHO KILLED THE POPE AND THE MESSIAH WHO THREATENED JEWISH CASTILE

Nicholas condemned Abulafia to be burned at the stake. Although the pope was finished with Abulafia, however, God apparently was not.

APPARENTLY, WHATEVER power resides in the lessons of history, there is greater power in the people's despair. When people suffer under intolerable conditions and can imagine only a single possible means of escape, they may need to believe in that means of escape, however unlikely or illogical. The Jewish Messiah myth itself was altered to accommodate this need. An oppressed and scattered Jewish people seized upon the theme of the birth pangs of the Messiah. This doctrine permitted a reactionary optimism—the worse things got, the more cause there was for hope. Thus, even after centuries of devastating failures, Jewish communities from time to time still needed to believe in the next Messiah, and a next Messiah always seemed to arise to fill this need.

If any Jewish community in the late Middle Ages could claim hardships sufficient to justify messianic longings, certainly the Spanish Jews would qualify. The Muslim invasion of Iberia in 711 had initially ushered in three centuries of a Jewish "golden age" when Jews were treated as a protected people and welcomed to participate in the arts, sciences, and commerce of the land. Then in the eleventh century the unity of the Muslim State dissolved, and the Christian monarchy of northern Spain (Castile and Aragon) gradually drove out the invaders. As has so often happened, the Jews were caught in the middle. Their special relationship with the forces in power vanished, and they were returned to their role, traditional in the Christian Middle Ages, as scapegoats for all of the economic, political, social, and even health problems of the society.

The Jewish condition in Spain steadily deteriorated, and by the thirteenth century, the Jews faced the beginnings of a terrible period of uncertainty, fear, torture, and slaughter. The Jewish community coped as best it could by such stratagies as conversion, practicing Judaism in secret, moving from the cities to the countryside, or fleeing the country. Another way in which the community coped was to make itself ready for the Messiah.

The first of the Spanish Messiahs of this era was an authentic scholar and major contributor to the development of Kabbalah, the central collection of Jewish mystical writings. His claims to be the Messiah received considerable support in Spain, Italy, Sicily, and Greece. His writings may have significantly influenced future

Jewish messianic figures. His most dramatic accomplishment was to be the only Jewish Messiah who killed a pope.

Abraham Abulafia was born in 1240 in Aragon, Spain, and grew up in Tuleda, Navarre. He came from a wealthy, privileged family, and had the additional advantage of being a child prodigy whose early mastery of Jewish learning led to a lifetime of significant writing. In particular, he contributed importantly to the development of early Kabbalistic concepts of the mystical meaning of the Hebrew alphabet (developed through *gematria*, the interpretation of words according to the numerical values of their letters) and the magical powers of the names of God.

Abulafia's messianic life had three phases, each preceded by a visionary call from God. His first call came in Barcelona in 1271, where he began teaching his divine vision to a small group of disciples. Abulafia thereupon followed his vision, traveling throughout the Mediterranean, studying, writing, and teaching. In Palestine, he set out to find the Sambatyon River, somewhere south of the Holy Land, beyond which the Ten Lost Tribes of Israel were said to reside while waiting to rejoin their Jewish brothers when the Messiah appears. (Although many of his followers believed that Abulafia had located the mythic river and met the Ten Tribes, it appears that he never got beyond Acre.)

But it was his second call, in 1280, that assured Abulafia of his unique place in the history of Jewish-Catholic relations. According to the most popular version of the story, in the midst of teaching and preaching to a growing group of followers in Capua, Italy, Abulafia had a vision in which God gave him a new mission. God told him to go to Pope Nicholas III and convert the pope to Judaism.

It is a mark of Abulafia's faith and sincerity that he promptly undertook this unpromising assignment. Abulafia's reputation as a religious scholar won him an audience with Pope Nicholas, but once the pope understood the purpose of the meeting, his reaction was predictable, swift, and harsh. Nicholas condemned

Abulafia to be burned at the stake. Although the pope was finished with Abulafia, however, God apparently was not.

Three days later, on August 22, 1280, it was not Abulafia but Pope Nicholas III who died. Nicholas was suddenly struck down by the plague. Abulafia was able to convince the Church authorities that this was not merely a random illness, but a divine intervention that rescinded the pope's order. The pope was buried, and Abulafia was released.[15]

He went on to Sicily to continue his studies and his teaching. In Messina, Sicily, Abulafia received his third and most elevating vision. God told Abulafia that he was, indeed, the Messiah who was about to lead the Jews to Jerusalem. After Abulafia's miraculous escape from the pope's death sentence, his followers were ready to accept him as the Messiah.

Abulafia and his followers also made much of the date of his birth—the year 1240 CE seemed special, since it corresponded with the year 5000 since Creation according to the Jewish calendar. Abulafia also adopted a popular prediction of the time for the Redemption as being 1290, one Jubilee (fifty years) after the fifth millennium from Creation. Since this was conveniently within his expected lifetime, his followers in the late 1280s prepared themselves for the Return to Jerusalem in the usual fashion—winding up or abandoning their business, selling their property, and preparing their wardrobe.

The skeptical reaction of Abulafia's doubters and opponents exceeded his followers' faithful acceptance. The leading Sephardi authority of the time, Rabbi Solomon ben Abraham Adret of Barcelona (the "Rashba"), so forcefully denounced Abulafia's messianic claims that a chastened Abulafia simply withdrew from actively promoting his claim to be the Messiah. Abulafia fled society to live on Comino (Kemmuna, one of the Maltese Islands), where he finished out his post-Messiah years writing additional important Jewish mystical books. The year 1290 did not bring the messianic Redemption that Abulafia had predicted. Instead, he died the next year, a Messiah who had inspired his followers and mortally triumphed over the pope, but who could not overcome the conservative opposition of the general Jewish community.

Spain's next Jewish Messiah was Nissim ben Abraham, the "Prophet of Avila," who declared his visions from God in 1295, in Avila, Castile. Following Mohammed's scenario, Nissim claimed to be illiterate, but said that he had been visited by an angel who dictated to him a book of mystical wisdom, on which Nissim had somehow been able to write extensive commentaries. When a summary of the book was sent to Rabbi Adret, the rabbi regarded it as no more than a compilation of common Christian prophetic works, and warned the Jewish community against following Nissim. This time the authority of the Rabbi of Barcelona proved powerless to prevent calamitous consequences for a gullible people.

When the Prophet of Avila predicted the specific day for the Redemption (on the last day of the Hebrew month of Tammuz, 1295), the people believed. In anticipation of the Messiah's appearance, the Jews of the area fasted and prayed. They finally gathered in their synagogues on the announced day, dressed in white gowns, ready to hear the blast of the ram's horn (shofar) that legend says will announce the Messiah's Coming.

No ram's horn was heard. No Messiah appeared. The people were devastated, and their resulting despair drove so many Jews to convert to Christianity that the continuity of the entire Jewish community in Castile was threatened.[16]

Thus, in the thirteenth century the Jews of Spain had put their faith in two very different Messiahs—a genteel scholar and an illiterate prophet—but the people's messianic yearnings were still unanswered. Still they were not deterred. If neither scholar nor prophet was to be their Messiah, then the Jews were ready to turn to a prince.

Chapter 9

THE MESSIAH PRINCE AND THE LAST IBERIAN MESSIAHS

Like the popular biblical heroes Joseph and Mordechai, Samuel Abulafia seemed second only to the king he served.

IF YOU want to be a Messiah, you can probably find some strand of Jewish messianic belief that fits your circumstances. Some sources say that the Messiah will appear as a poor man sitting among the beggars, a simple, humble man of the people. According to other sources the Messiah will be educated and wise, a privileged and powerful ruler, a prince. The Jews of Spain selected their next Messiah because he was a prince.

Samuel Abulafia of Castile (c. 1320–1361) never performed a miracle, never promised to lead the Jews back to the Holy Land, and never claimed to be a prophet or a Messiah. He did manage to reach a level of prince-like power, influence, and success in the court of Castile at a time when the Spanish Jews were confronted with a terrifying future of religious persecution. Because of the unprecedented station he achieved, it is not surprising that this prince of the people would be seized upon by many as the Messiah who would somehow be the agent of their salvation.

Samuel Abulafia was a wealthy financier who became a financial administrator and diplomat for King Don Pedro of Castile. Samuel's rewards for his services to the crown gained him an even greater fortune. He was revered in the Jewish community for his outstanding generosity and philanthropy, building synagogues in several cities (including the still surviving Toledo synagogue [1366], which became the Church of El Transito after the 1492 Expulsion). Samuel also built himself a magnificent personal residence, which today serves as the El Greco Museum in Toledo.

Samuel was treasurer and advisor to the king at a crucial time in the political development of Spain. The monarchy had not yet firmly established control over the powerful, independent noble families. In 1354, when the nobles mounted a serious revolt against the crown of Castile, Samuel played a major role in support of King Pedro. Samuel reformed the tax collection system and greatly strengthened the king's finances to support the war. When Pedro was victorious, he rewarded Samuel with some of the treasure confiscated from the rebel families. Samuel continued to rise in prominence. He was sent as a royal diplomat to Portugal in 1358.

Pedro treated Samuel Abulafia as a prince, and the Jews began to regard him as a Messiah. Like the popular biblical heroes Joseph and Mordechai, Samuel Abulafia seemed second only to the king he served. But Samuel had neglected one obvious cautionary sign: King Don Pedro had a nickname—"Pedro the Cruel"—and this did not promise a good working environment for the king's advisor. Perhaps Samuel had taught Pedro too well the financial benefits of wealth confiscation. In 1360 Pedro the Cruel arrested Samuel, had him tortured to death, and seized the great wealth of his former treasurer and his family. Samuel Abulafia made his final but involuntary contribution to the financial well being and centralization of power of the King of Castile.

The Spanish-Portuguese Messiah experience did not end with the successive failures of the Abraham Abulafia the scholar, Nissim ben Abraham the illiterate, and Samuel Abulafia the prince. The Messiah cycle simply began again. The next prominent Iberian Messiah was again a Jewish philosopher-writer-visionary who proclaimed himself the Messiah. Once again the appearance of this Messiah seems to be related to a time of deep troubles for the Jews. In this instance the triggering event may have been the bloody Spanish pogroms of 1391, which followed new anti-Jewish laws.

In 1393, Moses Botarel, a Kabbalistic scholar from Cisneros, Spain, declared in the city of Burgos that Elijah had visited him and had anointed him as the Messiah. Botarel authored a substantial but questionable body of literary works. Many of his books and pamphlets on the Bible and Kabbalah featured fabricated quotations falsely attributed to earlier real, or in some cases nonexistent, scholars. Botarel also implied that he had ghostwritten some books of the Christian philosopher Maestro Juan of Paris.

Botarel's prominence came in part from his writing, although even some contemporary writers recognized his literary frauds and attacked him for them. As for his status as a Messiah, although he apparently never developed a significant following or movement, Botarel's messianic claims became significant largely because a respected authority sponsored them—much as had happened 1,200 years earlier with Bar Kokhba. In the second century, the authority of Rabbi Akiba alone had been sufficient to legitimize Bar Kokhba's status as Messiah. At the end of the fourteenth century, one of the great Jewish philosophers of his time, Hasdai Crescus (1340–1410) similarly supported Moses Botarel's claims.

Regrettably, the ability of an academic fake to garner this support from such an eminent scholar appears to be the only significant miracle attributable to the Messiah Moses Botarel.

After this scholar-Messiah, a new uneducated Messiah appeared in Portugal in 1540. Ludovico (Luis) Diaz, "the Messiah of Setubal," was a poor, uneducated shoemaker who announced first that he was a prophet, and later that he was the Messiah. He was a Marrano (a member of a "New Christian" family of former Portuguese Jews who had converted, often under fear or force of the Inquisition[17]), and his lack of Jewish and general education meant that he did not preach important theological concepts. Diaz was able to win over his followers simply with the stories of his miracles.

The Marranos of Lisbon and Setubal (the nearby port city where Diaz was born), and even some Old Christians, believed in his miraculous powers and revered him as the Messiah. He was hailed as a king, with crowds swarming around to kiss his hand during his public appearances. This was not entirely a movement of the uneducated or superstitious lower class. His followers included Francisco Mendes, physician to Bishop Don Alfonso, and Gil Vaz Bugalho, a government official who secretly converted to Judaism and even wrote a manual of clandestine Jewish practices.

The open enthusiasm for Diaz in Lisbon made the end inevitable. The Inquisition arrested Diaz, but (as was common for a first offence) he was allowed to confess and recant his lapse into Judaising. After performing penance, he was released. Diaz stubbornly refused to stop his activities after his release, even though the standard Inquisition policy for a further relapse was death. The Inquisition rearrested the Messiah of Setubal and burned him at the stake in 1542, together with some 83 of his followers.

Chapter 10

THE ROLE OF WOMEN IN SPAIN'S MESSIAH STORIES

The importance of the Madonna image in Spanish-Catholic culture may have influenced Spanish Jews to seek a similar figure.

UNDER THE classical Jewish Messiah myth, the Messiah must be a male descendent of King David. With this job description it is not unexpected that (with the exception of Eva Frank, at the close of the eighteenth century, discussed in Chapter 21) women have generally played decidedly peripheral roles in the Jewish Messiah drama, primarily as wives and followers. A notable exception occurred in Spain and its colonies in the Americas in the late Middle Ages, when women figured significantly in the Jewish Messiah stories.

The importance of the Madonna image in Spanish-Catholic culture may have influenced Spanish Jews to seek a similar figure. The Conversos (descendants of Spanish Jews who had converted to Christianity during the times of the persecutions of the pogroms and Inquisition of the late fourteenth and fifteenth centuries) saw women as the prophets or potential mothers of the future Messiah.

The greatest heroine of the Spanish Jewish Messiah story was Ines, "the Maid of Herrera." A shoemaker's daughter, she lived in a substantial Converso community in northern Castile. At around 1500, Ines captivated the Converso community when she related her visions. In one dream, her deceased mother appeared and declared the importance of observing the obligations of charitable giving. In another dream Ines visited heaven and was assured that Elijah was about to announce the beginning of the messianic era. Thereafter the Messiah would appear and carry worthy Conversos to the Promised Land where all needs would be provided for (even Jewish bridegrooms for poor Converso girls without dowries).

Ines's message caused many followers to reconvert to Judaism, or at least to engage in fasting, Torah study, and Sabbath observance, even though Judaising was a capital offence under the Inquisition. This led to the end of the movement in 1501 when up to one hundred of her followers were found guilty of Judaising and were burned to death.

At about the same time as Ines of Herrera, a very similar story was being told about another Converso woman, Maria Gomez of Chillon, in Ciudad Real. Like Ines, Maria was also taken to heaven in a vision. She, too, received the promise that Conversos would have a place in the coming Redemption if they honored the Sabbath, fasted, and kept the other Torah commandments.

About one hundred years later, a Converso woman not only led her community in a return to Jewish observances, but also was widely believed to be the future mother of the Messiah. Dona Juana Enriquez was born in Seville, but emigrated to Mexico. She practiced many Jewish customs such as observing the Sabbath (by cooking ahead, dressing in fine clothes, and hosting communal meals), ritual bathing (mikvah), communal charity, and participating in funeral and condolence rituals. Unfortunately, the

Inquisition had emigrated to Mexico also, and Dona Juana's open Judaising had the expected result. She was imprisoned, tortured and publicly lashed.

Again, the story of this New World Converso was repeated in a similar tale. Followers of a Mexican-born Converso, Ines Pereira, likewise believed that she would be the mother of the Messiah.

The activities of these women marked the end of the early, often fragmentary tales of the Jewish Messiahs. With the coming of the sixteenth century, the story of the Jewish Messiahs arrived at its modern period. From here on, messianism was transformed by continual improvements in communications. This greatly broadened the scope of a Messiah's charismatic influence. On the other hand, community leadership opposed to messianic movements could now also express its views with increased sophistication and force. This combination of outspoken followers and outspoken opponents has given us some very vivid pictures of the modern Jewish Messiahs.

Chapter 11

THE FIRST ASHKENAZI MESSIAH

The center of Lemlein's movement remained in Venice, where Jews ignored their businesses and regular affairs and devoted much of the year to fasting and public self-flagellation.

SINCE THE first few centuries of Messiahs in the land of Israel, all the Messiahs had been Sephardi Jews, active in Spain, Portugal, Persia, Syria, or Yemen. The sixteenth century finally saw an enlargement of the scope of Jewish Messianic movements to include the other major group of world Jewry, the Ashkenazi Jews (Jews who had settled in Germany, Poland, Russia and Western Europe). The first of the Ashkenazi Messiahs was Asher Lemlein, born in Reutlingen, Germany, but active in Venice, Italy, around 1500–1502, where he studied Kabbalah.

The rabbis at this time were especially busy predicting various near-term dates for the appearance of the Messiah. There was much rabbinic authority for expecting the Messiah in 1500, and some prominent leaders also predicted dates of 1503 (Rabbi Isaac Abarbanel) or 1504 (Rabbi Abraham Zacuto). As always, such predictions stirred up the messianic expectations of the Jews, and in Lemlein's case may have influenced him to assume his messianic role.

In 1500, the young student Asher Lemlein announced that he was the prophet Elijah. He proclaimed that the Messiah would appear by 1502, provided that the Jews sufficiently repented and reformed. He was widely believed, not only in Italy, but also in the rest of Europe. Rabbi David Gans (1541–1613), a disciple of the famous Rabbi Judah Loew of Prague, related that his grandfather had demolished the special oven used each year for baking matzoh for Passover because he was so certain that Lemlein would lead the Jews back to Jerusalem before the next year. Then, as now, Jews ended their Passover Seder meal each year by declaring "Next year in Jerusalem!" Like so many other Jews at the outset of the sixteenth century, Rabbi Gans's grandfather was convinced that Asher Lemlein would finally make it happen.

Although it is not clear that Lemlein expressly claimed to be the Messiah, he did promise to lead the Jews in the Return. Many of his followers were sure that his announcement of the Messiah must refer to himself. Jews throughout Europe answered his call for charity, penitence, and fasting. The center of Lemlein's movement remained in Venice, where Jews ignored their businesses and regular affairs and devoted much of the year to fasting and public self-flagellation. The depth of the Jewish response caused the year 1502 to be called, by Jews and Christians alike, "The Year of Repentance."

When 1502 passed without the Messiah, the Jews were devastated. According to one version of the story, many of Lemlein's Venetian followers underwent baptism and conversion to Christianity. The reign of the first Ashkenazi Messiah abruptly ended.

Chapter 12

THE ODD COUPLE

Then, just as now, it would have been impossible even to imagine the fantastic truth about this procession.

IF YOU had been one of the lucky few in 1532 who happened to see that strange procession riding from Venice, Italy to Regensburg, Germany, you certainly would have taken notice. Initially, you would be impressed by the pageantry, of course, but then you would grow increasingly puzzled by some apparent contradictions. You first observe a small horseback troop elaborately dressed in fine silk livery, but you notice that they do not have an army escort. They are traveling under fluttering silk banners, but the markings on the flags are unrecognizable symbols—clearly not the usual heraldic tokens or royal crests from any of Italy's city-states. Your curiosity and attention naturally turn to seek the leader of the entourage. In this case, however, there seem to be two leaders, and it is hard to imagine a more mismatched pair.

Perhaps the first of these co-leaders to attract your eye is the handsome young man in his early thirties, riding with an air of calm determination. His bearing shows intelligence, education, and an easy confidence bred of a life in the royal court. You assume he must be a prince, but your assumption is both much too high and much too low.

As your gaze shifts to the other leader you feel a sense of shock at the contrast. This second man is riding the largest, most magnificent Arabian horse in the group, but the rider could not be similarly described. Well, "Arabian," perhaps. His skin is dark enough to place his origins somewhere in the Middle East or even Africa. But "large" and "magnificent" are not terms for this man. He is short and small—almost dwarf-like. It is difficult to guess his age; he might be close to fifty. He speaks in a strange language, and his demeanor suggests more of the desert than the palace.

That would probably have been the limit of what you could have observed as this splendid group passed by. Then, just as now, it would have been impossible even to imagine the fantastic truth about this procession.

Although the group is traveling without a regular army force, they actually carry very impressive protection. The leaders bear letters certifying that they are under the direct, personal protection of Pope Clement VII. The pope himself has sent these odd companions on this very delicate and important mission. They are going to meet with the Holy Roman Emperor Charles V to secure his cooperation in a final military campaign to achieve what over four hundred years of Christian Crusades have failed to accomplish—the recapture of the Holy Land and permanent expulsion of the Muslims from Jerusalem.

Who are these very special papal emissaries? The dark, gnome-like rider on the great white horse calls himself David Reuveni, a Jew, and since his sudden and mysterious appearance on the world stage almost a decade ago, he has excited both Christians and Jews throughout Europe and the Middle East with his story. This decidedly unmilitary-looking man has convinced much of the world that he is the general of a huge Jewish army of the legendary "Lost Tribes" of Israel (the ten tribes of the northern Kingdom of Israel which disappeared after being conquered and scattered by the Assyrians in 722 BCE). According to him, three hundred thousand mounted warriors are currently massed somewhere in Arabia, lacking only modern weapons to become a new military world force.

Reuveni has offered to lend his forces to Christendom's effort to regain the Holy Land. His stated motive is that restoring the Jews in Jerusalem will satisfy the last condition for the coming of the Messiah. Jews in many lands are convinced further that the remarkable David Reuveni himself must be the Messiah. They are sure that he only awaits the appropriate time to reveal himself after victory in Jerusalem.

And his companion on this quest? Once you accept, as Pope Clement has accepted, that Reuveni is about to bring on the messianic era, the role of his co-leader seems almost logical. The companion is the self-acknowledged Jewish Messiah. This is an unlikely role for anyone, but an especially unlikely one for the charismatic young man who now calls himself Shlomo (Solomon) Molkho. Before meeting Reuveni seven years ago, the Jewish Messiah Molkho was not Jewish and he was not the Messiah— indeed, he wasn't even Molkho.

Perhaps this odd couple—history's twin Jewish Messiahs—can be better understood if we try to unravel the twisted strands of their messianic lives.

Chapter 13

THE GENERAL OF THE PHANTOM ARMY

In the midst of the Inquisition, here was a Jew travelling from pope to king in exotic splendor and under banners emblazoned in Hebrew characters.

YOU MIGHT expect that history should be able to tell us at least the basic life story of someone who occupied, even briefly, the center of the world stage. If that is your expectation, then history fails with David Reuveni. He was certainly a major figure of the sixteenth century. He dealt with pope and king and emperor. He brought the world to the brink of a military campaign that was to have dwarfed the Crusades. His mission threatened to undo many of the forced conversions accomplished by the Portuguese Inquisition. He traveled in splendor and was accepted by many as the prophet of the messianic era, or perhaps as the Messiah himself. Yet history cannot tell us who he was, where he came from, or what finally happened to him. His life, to the extent we can know it, is like some uncharted comet, bursting suddenly and prominently into the world's view, quickly burning brighter, and then vanishing just as suddenly.

David Reuveni first appeared in 1523, when he was about forty years old. Historians cannot agree on his origins or background. Contemporaneous accounts often credited him with coming, as he himself claimed, from Arabia. Some modern historians suspect that he may have been one of the Jews of Ethiopia (the Beta Israel).[18] Some scholars have analyzed Reuveni's diary writings and concluded that he was a Polish Ashkenazi Jew. Other experts question whether Reuveni was even the author of his purported diary. Many agree that, whatever his origins, Arabs had captured Reuveni and held him as a slave until the Egyptian Jewish community in Alexandria eventually redeemed him.

When Reuveni arrived in Egypt in 1523, he failed to make much of a mark. This changed when he traveled on to the Holy Land. In Gaza, he began to gain popular support when he predicted the imminence of the messianic Redemption. At Hebron he fasted and prayed at the Cave of Machpelah, the burial place of Abraham and Sarah. He claimed to have caused there the miraculous refilling of the mikvah (ritual bath generally requiring some source of naturally flowing water) after years of drought. He went on to Jerusalem, praying and fasting at the Temple grounds and announcing to the Muslims there that he was their lord and the successor to Mohammed.

Reuveni also claimed that on the Jewish holiday of Shavuoth (Pentecost) in 1523, the force of his prayers turned the crescent moon atop the Dome of the Mosque so that it faced in a different direction. Reuveni took this as a divine portent that he should likewise travel in a different direction—that he should leave Muslim Jerusalem and go instead to the pope in Rome. In response to this sign, Reuveni went to Venice in 1524, where he obtained the assistance of some of the influential and wealthy members of the Jewish community in order to make his highly theatrical appearance in Rome.

Regardless of the truth of this background, Reuveni's startling appearance at the gates of the Vatican and the remainder of his active career for the next eight years are reasonably well documented. He appeared in Rome in 1524, riding a spectacular white Arabian horse, and accompanied by attendants dressed in fine silks.[19] He was dark skinned, thin, and short—some called him a dwarf. He spoke a strange language, which appeared to be a mixture of Arabic and some variant of Hebrew. Whatever this language was, it was sufficient for Reuveni to tell such a wondrous tale that he not only obtained an audience with Pope Clement VII, but managed to earn the pope's confidence and support.

David Reuveni told the pope that he was the younger brother of Joseph, the hereditary head of the tribe of Reuven (hence David Reuveni's name). Joseph ruled as King of the Lost Tribes of Israel. David Reuveni himself was the general of the combined army from the tribes of Reuven, Gad, and half of Manasseh (the tribes that in biblical times occupied land east of the Jordan River, rather than in Israel proper), which was standing by somewhere in Arabia. Reuveni assured the pope that the army awaited only modern weapons to become the force that could retake the Holy Land from the Ottoman Sultan Suleiman I ("Suleiman the Magnificent") and the Muslim Turks, thereby bringing on the coming of the Messiah.

This was all that Pope Clement needed to hear. For over four hundred years the Christian world's Crusades had been unable to take and hold Jerusalem. Now Reuveni offered a new military strategy. The Jewish force would attack the Turks from the rear while the Christians would mount a final frontal assault. The Muslims would be caught in a classic pincer action. This pope would accomplish what seventy-seven of his predecessors had failed to do.

The pontiff was not concerned that he would be advancing the

Jewish messianic cause. Church theology generally recognized that the Jewish biblical conditions for the coming of the Messiah (including the restoration of the Jews to the Holy Land) must be fulfilled as a prerequisite to Jesus' Second Coming and the universal End of Days for all mankind.

Reuveni's story of the army of the Lost Tribes did not seem so outlandish in the mid-sixteenth century. It was universally known that all the Jews then living in the known world were descendants of the two tribes from the southern Kingdom of Judah. Over the centuries, rumors and reports persisted that some part, at least, of the vanished ten tribes of the northern Kingdom of Israel had managed to remain intact, living in some remote part of the world—Arabia, Ethiopia, Yemen, or elsewhere.

The failure of the Lost Tribes to make contact with the rest of the world in the previous twenty-three centuries was seen as logically explainable by the fact that, even in the sixteenth century, many parts of the world were still isolated and unexplored. The legend surrounding the Lost Tribes, accepted at that time by Christians as well as Jews, provided a more poetic reason for the Tribes' continued isolation. According to the legend, the Ten Lost Tribes were living behind the great Sambatyon River, which God had rendered impassible in order to save the Ten Tribes until the time arrived for the Restoration.

An additional basis for Christian acceptance of Reuveni's story came from another popular legend. In Pope Clement's time, most of the Christian world believed various reports concerning the mysterious Prester John. This mythical Christian priest and king purportedly had written letters to several popes describing how he ruled over a large territory in Africa, where he had amassed fabulous wealth and converted many native tribes to the Church. Since some of these reports said that Prester John had made contact with—or perhaps had battled—the Lost Tribes of Israel, it was a case of one myth verifying another.

In short, after a year or so of contemplating Reuveni's proposal, Pope Clement gave him letters of safe passage to Portugal, to meet with King John III. Unlike the Vatican, Portugal carried on trading activities with the Arabian Peninsula, so perhaps the pope felt that King John had special knowledge about that part of the world and would be better able to authenticate Reuveni's story. Reuveni was also to seek John's commitment to join the Jewish-Christian campaign to recapture Jerusalem. Reuveni may have had his large Jewish army, but he needed to secure modern Portuguese armament and ships if his warriors were to be effective against the Muslims.

Reuveni's mission in Portugal started exceptionally well. He arrived in 1526 and made a triumphal procession to see the king. The adulation of the crowds, especially of the Marranos, is understandable. In the midst of the Inquisition, here was a Jew travelling from pope to king in exotic splendor and under banners emblazoned in Hebrew characters. It was acknowledged that he came as the general of the great army of the Lost Tribes, and that his task was nothing less than to bring about the beginning of the messianic era. Many believed that he was more than just the messenger of the Messiah—surely he must be the Messiah himself, and would begin his reign after his great victory in Jerusalem.

Although Reuveni's official story was that he was only the general of the Jews, and not the Messiah, he took several contradictory steps that fostered the popular belief that he was the Messiah. He told his miracle stories of Hebron and Jerusalem. He also took care to trace his lineage to Solomon, King David's son (also explaining why he chose David as his first name). By making these two elements part of his personal history, Reuveni was appropriating very important elements of the standard Jewish Messiah story—the power to work miracles, and Davidic descent.

Initially, the Portuguese religious and civil powers accepted Reuveni with almost the same enthusiasm that the Marranos exhibited. He stayed at the home of the king's brother, Cardinal Don Enrique. After Reuveni's first meetings with King John, the king not only endorsed his mission, but promised substantial military support, including eight ships and four thousand canon to arm the Jewish warriors. John treated Reuveni as if he were someone between the level of an important diplomat and a visiting head of state. Success was almost within Reuveni's grasp. But then the king made one more diplomatic gesture of hospitality that proved to be the ruin of Reuveni's Portuguese hopes. John suspended the Inquisition trials during Reuveni's visit.

The Marranos, emboldened by this sudden theological détente, now flocked to see Reuveni. Ever increasing throngs declared their loyalty to him. Whatever the Christians may have thought about who would be entitled to share in the benefits to be brought by the Messiah, one aspect of the standard Jewish Messiah myth was far from universalistic. Many rabbis had taught that the messianic era would also bring a reversal of the Jews' temporal fortunes, so that when the Jews were gathered to the Holy Land, Israel would be reestablished as the first among the world's nations. Thus it is understandable that, in response to Reuveni's promise that the messianic era was beginning, many Marranos announced themselves ready to readopt the Judaism of their ancestors in order to be included in the nation that would soon rule the world.

The king accused Reuveni of using his mission in order to reconvert the Marranos. Reuveni denied this, but there was one reconversion that he couldn't discourage and couldn't deny. The king's own council secretary, Diogo Pires, had visions announcing that Pires was the Messiah whose reign would be established by Reuveni. Although Reuveni refused to help Pires, he could not stop him. When Pires declared himself to be the Jewish Messiah Shlomo Molkho, Reuveni was forced to leave Portugal without achieving any of his goals.

Reuveni then went through several years of wanderings that did little to advance his own cause except to inflame further messianic fever among the Jews. First, he was captured and imprisoned in Spain, but won eventual release. Bad luck continued to dog his travels, and next he was shipwrecked off the coast of Provence and imprisoned there for two years. This time his freedom had to be purchased by ransom paid to the King of France by the Jewish communities of Avignon and Carpentras.

Reuveni finally returned to Italy in 1530, but his great popularity with some elements of the Italian Jewish population was not matched by similar acceptance by the civil and Church powers. Thus, whatever his real feelings may have been in 1532 (his diary ends just after the release from Spanish prison), he accepted a new assignment from the pope, even though it linked him together again with Shlomo Molkho.

This new (and it turns out, last) mission for Pope Clement was even more daunting than the negotiations with King John. This time Reuveni, traveling together with Molkho, was to seek the participation of Charles V, the Holy Roman Emperor, in Reuveni's plan for a joint Jewish-Christian military attack to retake Jerusalem.

When the twin emissaries approached Charles at Regensburg, where the imperial council was meeting, Charles provided Reuveni a reception far different from the one initially extended by the hospitable and accepting King John of Portugal. Reuveni and Molkho were promptly imprisoned.

Some believe that the emperor's response was due to a warning from Fredrick, the Marquis of Mantua, that Reuveni's papers from the pope were forgeries (perhaps created to replace the original documents that Reuveni had lost in his shipwreck and imprisonment). Other evidence points to the active intervention of Hieronymous Aleander, papal emissary in Germany, who secretly subverted his pontiff's plan to recapture Jerusalem because he felt it could only end badly—either there would be disaster for the

Church if the military campaign failed, or else glory for the Jews if it were successful.

Charles sent Reuveni in chains to be tried by the Inquisition in Spain. The details of David Reuveni's end are not clear. Some experts claim that he escaped or perhaps won his release by agreeing to convert. Others conclude that the Inquisition immediately killed him, or the Spanish government imprisoned him and eventually killed him several years later.

This master storyteller first appeared suddenly on the world stage without a personal history other than the one he created for himself. For a few years, Reuveni was on the verge of convincing the rulers of Christendom to furnish arms and ships for his mythical army of the Lost Tribes, and to rely on his ability to lead this army in a joint military campaign to retake Jerusalem. Then he disappeared as mysteriously as he began.

Chapter 14

THE MESSIAH WHO WAS SAVED BY THE POPE

Fortunately, once Pope Clement was convinced of a Jewish Messiah, he did not display his support half-heartedly. At the last moment, Clement personally saved Molkho from execution in a most extraordinary manner.

A JEWISH Messiah pursues a high-risk occupation. Most Messiahs' lives ended early at the hands of the Christian, Muslim, or civil authorities. A disbelieving or frightened Jewish community blocked others. Only a few Messiahs died in their beds. After all, when it is a Messiah who is threatened, who else could be powerful enough to save him? Shlomo Molkho found the answer. He so impressed Pope Clement VII as being a true Messiah that the Pope secretly saved Molkho after the Church's own Inquisition sentenced him to death.

Shlomo Molkho was born Diogo Pires in Lisbon, in 1500, to a family of Portuguese Marranos. At the time of David Reuveni's triumphal papal mission to Portugal in 1525, Pires held an important scribal position in the court of King John III, serving as secretary to the king's council and court recorder for the royal court of appeals. Pires and Reuveni met when Reuveni appeared before King John to seek support for his plan to reconquer the Holy Land.

Like many other Marranos, Pires believed that Reuveni was about to lead the army of the Lost Tribes of Israel to retake Jerusalem from the Turks, an act that would usher in the messianic era. But Pires's response to Reuveni went far beyond simply developing hope for the messianic era, or even believing that Reuveni might ultimately turn out to be the Messiah. Instead, Pires's own visions and dreams told him that Reuveni's battle would establish Pires as the Messiah. His visions directed Pires to adopt Judaism, undergo circumcision, and travel to Turkey.

When Pires asked Reuveni to circumcise him, Reuveni refused. This didn't stop Pires. That night, Pires circumcised himself, adopted Judaism, and renamed himself Shlomo Molkho ("Shlomo" from the Hebrew name for Solomon, King David's son, again referring to the Davidic lineage that was a classical requirement for the Messiah, and "Molkho" from the Hebrew "melech," meaning "king").

Molkho's act of self-circumcision was more than just an initiation rite for his becoming Jewish, or even a remarkable demonstration of the sincerity of his conviction. The act became the first significant element in his history as a Jewish Messiah. Several familiar bible stories center on circumcisions involving special people: Abraham (who initiated the ritual of circumcision as a sign of God's covenant with the Jewish people), Jacob's sons (who revenged their sister's rape while Shechem and his followers were recuperating from circumcision), and Moses (who was a principal participant in a mysterious biblical circumcision story). Molkho's circumcision identified him with these biblical heroes.

Jewish circumcision also has a significant messianic sub-text.

Jewish custom teaches that the prophet Elijah, the advance
messenger of the Messiah, is present in spirit at every
circumcision ceremony. Continuing through today, a chair is set
aside as "Elijah's Chair" at the circumcision ceremony. (Some
take this folk custom as saying, in effect, that every male Jew has
the potential to be the Messiah.)

Finally, Molkho turned the act of self-circumcision into the
first of several miracles authenticating his status as Messiah. In his
autobiographical writings, Molkho reported that God
miraculously healed him "in an unbelievably short time."

Whatever the level of divine involvement, it was obvious that the
notorious conversion of a high-level functionary in the king's court
was politically unwise. Like Reuveni, Molkho also had to flee
Portugal in 1525, but at this point their paths separated for a time.

Shlomo Molkho began a seven-year personal odyssey traveling
through southern Europe, living a pure and ascetic life, studying
Kabbalah, and preaching to Jews and Christians. Kabbalah is a
very deep and esoteric body of mystical writings about the nature
of God and the role of man in the universe. Although mastery of
these materials generally takes many years of difficult study,
Molkho's popular sermons on Kabbalah began very soon after his
conversion. His followers cited the ability of this neophyte scholar
to become a great teacher of Kabbalah so quickly as an additional
miracle supporting Molkho's claim to be the Messiah. (Some—
but not all—modern historians explain the same phenomenon by
assuming that, like some other Marranos who had not fully lost
interest in Judaism, Molkho had probably secretly studied
Judaism and the Kabbalah as a young man.)[20]

We are not certain of Molkho's exact route through Europe, but
we do know that he eventually found his way to the city of
Salonika (Thessaloniki), an important business center on the
Adriatic coast then under Turkish rule. In the mid-sixteenth
century, Salonika was a major Jewish population site, especially

for Sephardi Jews who had fled the Inquisition or had suffered forced emigration under the Jewish expulsions decreed by Spain (1492) and Portugal (1497). In Salonika, Shlomo Molkho continued his studying and preaching, gaining many disciples and followers. He published a collection of his sermons there emphasizing the approaching Redemption. Molkho believed that the sack of Rome in 1527 satisfied one of the predicted preconditions of the coming of the final messianic era, the upset of the ruling civil authority. He predicted that his messianic reign would begin in a few years, by 1540.

While he lived in Salonika, Molkho also met and impressed the great Jewish teacher and writer, Rabbi Joseph Karo. Karo was himself influential in the development of Kabbalah, and subsequently also became a Jewish Messiah figure in his own right (discussed in Chapter 15).

Apparently the leaders of Salonika's Jewish community became alarmed at the enthusiasm now swirling around Molkho and his claims to be the Messiah. Such a situation raised more than internal theological issues. The entire Jewish community might suffer if the ruling Muslim Turkish government felt threatened by religious turmoil. The concerns of the Jewish community forced Molkho to leave Salonika, and in 1529 he went on to Italy, where he began the high period of his life as a Messiah.

He started out in Ancona, Italy, by continuing his practice of preaching to growing crowds of Jews and Christians. Once again, his popularity created a problem, this time because stories began to circulate that he was a Marrano who had reconverted (a capital offence under the Inquisition). He eventually went on to Rome, where he managed to make an entrance almost as dramatic as David Reuveni's earlier arrival.

While Reuveni had entered dressed in fine silks and riding a great white horse, Molkho orchestrated his own appearance to achieve exactly the opposite effect. One of the Talmudic descriptions of the Messiah relates how the Messiah will appear as a miserable beggar sitting among the poor and sick at the gates of the city.[21] Much in the spirit of some modern American political candidates who embellish stories of their poor and simple origins so as to fit within the Lincoln myth, Molkho determined to satisfy this rabbinic prediction for the Messiah.

Molkho wrote how he rode into Rome with his usual fine clothes and banners decorated with magical names and symbols. Then, in order to fit into the legend of how the Messiah would appear, he left all that finery with his innkeeper. Instead, he blackened his face with dirt and dressed in filthy rags. In this unaccustomed uniform, Molkho went to the Tiber Bridge near the pope's Castle San Angelo, where he stayed for thirty days, living with the sick and poor beggars and not touching meat or wine.

Pope Clement VII had been convinced just a few years earlier that David Reuveni was the general of a huge army of the Lost Tribes of Israel. It is not surprising, therefore, that Clement would also believe that Shlomo Molkho, this beggar sitting at his gates, was the Jewish Messiah he claimed to be. Like many other Christians and Jews in Rome, Clement was especially impressed by the miraculous prophesies Molkho announced. Molkho's visionary dreams enabled him to predict that there would soon be major flooding in Rome (which occurred on October 8, 1530), that there would be an earthquake in Portugal (which occurred in January, 1531), and that a great comet would appear (which occurred with the arrival of Halley's comet in 1531).

Despite his support by the pope, Molkho was not yet safe in Rome. When Molkho's history of being a reconverted Marrano followed him to Rome, the Inquisition sentenced him to death by burning at the stake, the standard punishment for the crime of Judaising by lapsed New Christians.[22] Fortunately, once Pope Clement was convinced of a Jewish Messiah, he did not display his support half-heartedly. At the last moment, Clement personally saved Molkho from execution in a most extraordinary manner. Clement hid Molkho in the Vatican chambers and substituted another victim to be burned in Molkho's place so that the Inquisition's body count for the day would not be incomplete. The pope's remarkable intervention not only spared Molkho's life but also added to his legend. Molkho's followers accepted the news of this fantastic escape as yet another miracle confirming that Molkho was the Messiah.

Where could he go from here? Even with the pope's protection, Molkho's practice of preaching to Jews and Christians in Italy had become too dangerous under the constant threat of the Inquisition. The earlier fear and concern of the Jewish leaders in Salonika had demonstrated that Molkho could not find refuge even in a strong Jewish community where he might develop a large following. The option that remained available to him would not turn out to be much of an improvement.

Shlomo Molkho now joined up with David Reuveni in Venice, and together they rode to Regensburg to convince Charles V, the Holy Roman Emperor, to participate in the David Reuveni-Pope Clement plan for a joint Jewish-Christian Holy War to regain Jerusalem.

This was not a wise move. Charles reacted decisively to these two Jewish dreamers (or schemers)—one who promised an army of three hundred thousand men that no one else had ever seen, and the other who claimed to be the Messiah. The emperor sent Reuveni to the Inquisition in Spain, but returned Molkho, the Messiah, in chains to Mantua for his Inquisition trial. There Molkho was once again sentenced to be burned at the stake.

This time there was no miraculous last-minute intervention by the pope.[23] The emperor gave Molkho one final opportunity to avoid the death sentence. Charles offered Molkho a reprieve and a permanent position in the emperor's court if Molkho would renounce his claim to be the Messiah and convert to Christianity.

Shlomo Molkho, guided to the end by his visions, refused. He was burned to death in Mantua in 1532.

His role as Messiah survived Molkho's death in several respects. The Jewish Messiah legend taught that two Messiahs will appear: a failed military Messiah of the House of Joseph, followed by a successful spiritual leader, the Messiah of the House of David. Under this legend the death of a Messiah is not necessarily inconsistent with his authenticity. Perhaps Molkho chose death rather than conversion not simply because he believed he was the Messiah, but because he believed that his death would fulfill the requirement of an initial Messiah of the House of Joseph. In this way, he could bring the Jews and the entire world one step closer to universal Redemption.

As can be seen in many other stories of Messiahs before and after Molkho (and echoing the Gospels of Jesus), many of Molkho's followers were also certain that their Messiah could not have died. There were rumors that Molkho had somehow miraculously escaped. There were stories that he had died but had been or soon would be resurrected. And there were reports solemnly testifying that he had reappeared for a week, was seen by several people during that time, and only later mysteriously disappeared. Many other followers accepted the fact of Molkho's death but saw its nobility as confirming his sincerity and even holiness. Rabbi Joseph Karo, who had met Molkho earlier in Salonika, later expressed his own longing for such a holy death.

Molkho's followers lovingly preserved and revered as holy relics the Messiah's fine silk clothing and flag with the mysterious letters and symbols. The Pinkas Synagogue in Prague maintained these garments for centuries. (If you wish to experience a personal encounter with your messianic heritage, you can see Molkho's silk tunic and flag still on display today in the Jewish Museum of Prague.) Soon after Molkho's death these garments were said to embody powerful magical qualities, and, as we shall see, their legend was appropriated a century later to confirm the authenticity of the Jewish Messiah Shabbatai Zevi.

Jews today still recount Shlomo Molkho's story with reverence, especially in the Sephardi community. A contemporary elementary Hebrew language instruction course-book even uses a story about Molkho's romantic letter to a young woman in the city of Safed as a modern language exercise. Scholars also generally credit Molkho for having delivered intelligent, powerful sermons that influenced many listeners of the time to embrace a life of increased religious purity and zeal.

The nature of Molkho's life as a Messiah makes it impossible to use the popular term "false Messiah" to describe him. Obviously, his life did not mark the immediate arrival of the messianic era. He was, in this sense, a failed Messiah, as indeed all Jewish Messiahs have been to date. But at least one historian has recognized Molkho as being in his time the most influential Jewish Messiah since Jesus.[24] The purity of Molkho's life, the apparent sincerity of his belief, the quality and consequences of his theology, and the martyrdom of his death have all earned Shlomo Molkho the right to be called, simply, a Jewish Messiah.

Chapter 15

THE KABBALIST MESSIAHS

Many Jewish Messiahs have struggled with internal conflict, but seldom has there been as contradictory a Messiah as Joseph Karo.

THE FIFTEENTH century was the inaugural century of the Spanish Inquisition. The institution, and related pogroms, soon proved to be efficient and effective. By the 1490s, the majority of the Jews of Spain and Portugal had been killed, fled the country, or converted to become "New Christians" (although a substantial number of the Converso and Marrano families retained some Jewish observances for many generations). The dilemma of the remaining Iberian Jews—whether to continue living under fear and oppression, or to flee their homeland—was resolved for them by the Spanish and Portuguese governments.

At the same time that King Ferdinand and Queen Isabella of Spain sent Christopher Columbus on his way, they also sent the Jews on their way, although in a strikingly different manner. The king and queen gave Columbus three ships. They gave the Jews three months. Under the March 31, 1492, Order of Expulsion, any Jews found in Spain after June 1492 would be killed. So many

Spanish Jews (perhaps 150,000) fled to Portugal that Portugal followed with its own Expulsion Order in 1497.

The crown gave Columbus royal financing for his journey, but prohibited the Jews from taking even their own wealth or property with them. Despite this confiscatory legislation, the Sephardi Jews fleeing Spain and Portugal were able to take with them something of unique value.

Fifteen centuries earlier, Jews exiled from the land of Israel to Babylonia had carried with them the treasure of the Torah. This enabled them to subsequently develop the elaborate rabbinic commentaries of the Talmud. A parallel arose for Spanish and Portuguese Jews. Beginning in the thirteenth century, the Jews of Iberia had written the Zohar and other basic books of Jewish mystical thought comprising the foundation of Kabbalah. The new exile generation now brought this treasure with them on their flight from Spain and Portugal.[25] After settling in the Holy Land and the Middle East, the Iberians and their descendents subsequently developed these fundamental works of the Kabbalah into the modern sophisticated doctrines of Kabbalah that still dominate Kabbalistic philosophy and practice today.

In light of the intensely esoteric, mystical doctrines developed in post-Iberian Kabbalah, it is not surprising that some of the principal contributors to this intellectual process also generated messianic movements. The earliest of the Kabbalist-Messiahs was Rabbi Joseph Karo (1488–1575). Born in Toledo, Castile, he and his family fled Spain at the time of the 1492 Expulsion. Like many others, they first sought refuge in Portugal, but after the 1497 Portuguese Expulsion, Karo and his family settled in Istanbul. He later also lived in Adrianople, Nikopol (Bulgaria), and Salonika.

Many Jewish Messiahs have struggled with internal conflict, but seldom has there been as contradictory a Messiah as Joseph Karo. He was both the ultimate traditionalist scholar who interpreted normative Jewish law, and the ultimate mystic visionary who lived a life of continual occult experiences.

Karo began his studies with his father, Ephraim Karo, a noted Talmudic scholar. This early education prepared Karo for a life of rigorous Talmudic study and writing. Indeed, even if Karo had never been involved with the development of Kabbalah or his own Messiah claims, he would still be renowned as one of the greatest Jewish authors for his *Shulhan Arukh*. Traditional Jews today still recognize this exhaustive codification of Jewish law and practice as authoritative.

Joseph Karo was also one of the first of the important post-Expulsion contributors to the development of the mystical doctrines of Kabbalah, particularly in his elaboration of the concept of the Shekhinah (the spirit of God, generally as a feminine aspect). As already noted, Karo was an early champion of Shlomo Molkho, whom he met and proclaimed to be the anointed Messiah. After Molkho heroically chose death in 1532 rather than convert, Karo expressed how he yearned for holy martyrdom like Molkho's.

Joseph Karo did not merely vicariously live in the mystical experiences of others, such as those of Shlomo Molkho. Karo personally lived a lifetime of such experiences. A divine spirit (maggid) regularly visited Karo throughout his fifty-year active career, instructing him in the secrets of Kabbalah and the ideals of ascetic living. Karo maintained a diary detailing these visitations, and also recorded their teachings in various Kabbalistic works.

In addition, Karo repeatedly experienced the phenomenon of automatic speech—his divine visitor audibly spoke through him, sometimes in the presence of others. Karo was conscious during this automatic speaking, so he was also later able to record these incidents in his diary. Karo believed in his spirit's messages, and they told him that he was destined to be the Messiah. Despite this, the messianic aspects of his spirit-mentor's teachings did not lead to the establishment of any significant messianic movement centering on Karo.

To the contrary, many of Karo's disciples and followers in the Jewish intellectual community were embarrassed by Karo's reports of his mystical encounters and his claims to be the Messiah. When a portion of Karo's handwritten diary was finally published almost a century after his death (*Maggid Mesharim*, 1646), the publisher reorganized the diary material into the form of more typical biblical commentary. Even after this unauthorized editing, some readers still refused to accept that the author of the revered *Shulhan Arukh* could have written these accounts of divine visitations.

The result of this community resistance is that Joseph Karo's messianic claims remain only a footnote to the record of his significant contributions to the codification of Judaic practice and the development of modern Kabbalah. We remember his unrealized role as a Messiah only as a precursor of two major Kabbalist Messiahs who followed him.

The stories of these later Kabbalist Messiahs—and the story of the post-Expulsion development of modern Kabbalah generally—are centered in the city of Safed, in the mountains of northern Palestine. After the 1492 Expulsion from Spain, many rabbis and mystics settled in Safed. Their choice was not coincidental. The city was near the graves of several important masters of biblical commentary, as well as the cave where, according to legend, Rabbi Shimon bar Yohai composed the basic Zohar while he hid from the Romans for seventeen years. There was even a tradition that the Messiah would first appear in the upper Galilee. This expectation found fulfillment in the next Kabbalah Masters.

The first Messiah to appear in Safed was the greatest of the Kabbalah masters, Isaac Luria Ashkenazi (1534–1572), known as the "Ari" (lion). Luria and his disciples shaped Kabbalah into its present form. Born in Jerusalem, he studied the Zohar in Egypt with the greatest authority of the time, Rabbi Moshe Cordovero.

Luria didn't settle in Safed until 1570, just two and a half years before his death. He wrote no books and gave only occasional public sermons. Instead he taught disciples, primarily while strolling around the Safed area. With those two and a half years of peripatetic instruction, Luria was able to develop several of the basic themes of contemporary Kabbalah and inspire a group of students and disciples to record and elaborate on his thoughts.

Luria's philosophical innovations included the theory that each soul is comprised of elements of the souls of several earlier persons, and the theory that the Messiah would come when all Jews participated in the repair (tikun) of the imperfect world by their universal observance of the biblical commandments (mitzvot). The force of the tikun concept has been so overwhelming that, when we speak generally of Kabbalah today, we are usually referring to Lurianic Kabbalah.

Luria's philosophical concepts also had impact upon his personal Messiah movement. While everyone's soul contains fragments of predecessors' souls, Luria concluded that his soul incorporated elements from several famous biblical and rabbinic personages. Luria taught that even the Messiah couldn't bring about the messianic era unless the people unite in strict and complete observance of their biblical duties. Thus, Luria implied that he could be the true Messiah and yet not be successful in bringing on utopia.

Many of Luria's followers, and probably Luria himself, believed that he was the true Messiah. As usual, the people were ready for the Return. The hardships and displacement of the Expulsion certainly seemed sufficient to satisfy the prediction that the appearance of the Messiah would be preceded by birth pangs. And of course, there were the miracles.

Luria's life was permeated with miracles. On his eighth day, he was circumcised by an invisible (except to his father) Elijah, the prophet of the Messiah. In an echo of Shlomo Molkho, Luria healed miraculously quickly. He was (like Jesus and several of the Jewish Messiahs) a child prodigy. At the funeral of his mentor, Cordovero, Luria alone saw a great pillar of cloud, marking Luria as successor to his teacher, and recalling God's appearance to Moses and the Israelites in the Exodus. Luria could read the secret condition of people's bodies and souls by viewing or touching them. He knew the unmarked locations of the graves of the great writers of the Talmud, and (in a manner recalling the actions of the prophets Elijah and Elisha) he communed with the spirits of the deceased by stretching out on their graves. He received spiritual revelations, and (like Moses) his face glowed when he did. Luria also correctly predicted the death of his son and his own death, which occurred from the plague in 1572.

Even if all of this had not been sufficient to establish a messianic movement around Isaac Luria, he also enjoyed one final messianic advantage—his principal disciple, Hayim Vital Calabrese (1542–1620). Vital, who generally controlled the Luria legend after the Ari's death, was not bashful about asserting that Luria had been a Messiah of the House of Joseph—the unsuccessful Messiah destined to die without fulfilling the messianic promise because the people were not yet ready. It may not be surprising, then, that Vital saw himself as the next Messiah, succeeding his teacher in this as well as in the leadership of the Kabbalah scholarship community.

Born in Safed, Vital studied and was ordained as a rabbi in Jerusalem. The fact of his ordination itself may offer an interesting measure of the messianic fervor of the times. Judaism had suspended formal ordination in the fourth (some say as late as the eleventh) century. The rabbis had only recently reinstituted the practice, in part because such formalities had once again become important under the sixteenth century's expectation of the Messiah. Vital went on to teach and preach in Israel, Syria, and

Egypt. Upon joining with Luria in Safed, Vital became his principal pupil and confidant.

Vital had more of a basis for his claim to be the successor Messiah than just being Luria's protégé in studying Kabbalah. Vital had studied and written on his own about magic and alchemy. He, too, communed with the spirits of dead scholars. He recorded the details of a visitation from Elijah and their journey together to heaven where God promised Vital the seat at God's right-hand side. Vital also related other visions confirming the divine promise that he was the Messiah who would finally bring about the Restoration.

Because Luria left no writings, Vital was crucial in the documentation and interpretation of Lurianic Kabbalah. Compared to the lasting appreciation of these Kabbalistic works, there is little current awareness that Vital was also responsible for establishing the claims of both Luria and himself as the Messiahs (together with Karo) of the Kabbalistic movement.

Chapter 16

THE RABBI WHO BECAME CHRISTIANITY'S EXPERT ON THE MESSIAH

Cromwell had to be convinced to readmit Jews to England in order to satisfy the last condition to the appearance of the Messiah. The most bizarre aspect of this scheme was that it actually worked.

YOU MIGHT think that the last thing Christianity needed in the seventeenth century was a rabbi to tell them about the Messiah. Christians already had their Messiah. They had Jesus. But Christians still needed to bring about the conditions necessary for Jesus' Second Coming. That's where the rabbi came in.

The birth of Protestantism in the mid-sixteenth century brought to Christianity a new spirit of religious intellectual independence. Protestants discarded centuries of mandated biblical interpretation by the Catholic Church and returned to the sources—in this case, the early translations of the Hebrew

Bible—to learn the truth for themselves. As Protestants began reading the Hebrew Bible and commentaries, it didn't take them long to catch Jewish Messiah fever.

Especially appealing to the Protestants was the theme that the messianic utopia would be preceded by the birth pangs of the Messiah. The Protestant Revolution itself and the Thirty Years' War (1618–1648) had both engulfed all Europe, and seemed to satisfy the requirement of a period of chaos and destruction before the messianic era. To Jews this meant that a Jewish Messiah was about to appear, but to Christians this meant that the Second Coming was near.

The Protestants were convinced by their study of Jewish sources that additional conditions for the Messiah must be met. Christians agreed that a Jewish Messiah of the Davidic line must appear (not, of course, as a divine competitor of Jesus, but as a national leader who would unify the world in peace and set the stage for Jesus' return). In addition the Jews must be restored to their homeland in the land of Israel. This did not mean only some Jews. To bring about the Second Coming, Protestants were convinced that (as promised in the Hebrew Bible) the Return must include all the Jews scattered throughout the four corners of the world—both the Jews that were known, and the Ten Lost Tribes of Israel.

It remained an article of Jewish faith, accepted by Christians also, that the Ten Tribes continued to exist intact, ready for their necessary participation in the Return. The only question was, where were they? Over the centuries, repeated travelers' reports of sightings and contacts had placed the Tribes in Persia, Arabia, Yemen, India, and Africa. There were scarcely enough Lost Tribes to go around.[26]

The various travelers' reports that had kept the legend of the Lost Tribes alive in the seventeenth century raised their own question. With all this supposed contact, how could the Lost Tribes continue to be lost? The legend itself provided the solution:

the Ten Tribes were separated from the inhabited world by the Sambatyon River.

The Sambatyon would have earned its place in world renown merely from its impressive size. It was seventeen miles wide. But its most interesting characteristic was its weekly schedule. The Sambatyon was the world's only river that observed the Sabbath. On six days of the week, the river ran fiercely, with huge, tumbling rocks and turbulent sand making it impassible. On Saturdays, the Jewish Sabbath (perhaps the source of the river's name), the river was quiet. As everyone knew, Jews were not permitted to travel on the Sabbath. This had resulted in the Ten Tribes' total separation from the rest of the world for the prior two millenia.[27]

All this had been confirmed for the seventeenth century by the fresh reports of Gershon ben Eliezer, who told of finding the Sambatyon River during his 1630 travels in India. Besides such "eye-witness" accounts, the river's Sabbath schedule was not only recounted in the rabbinic literature, but had also been described as established fact in the first century *Natural History* of Pliny the Elder and in Josephus's history, *The Jewish War*.[28]

The Christian world had to solve the riddle of the Sambatyon River and find the Ten Lost Tribes in order to prepare the way for the Second Coming. The Protestants felt that they needed expert advice, so they turned to the seventeenth century rabbi famous to both Jews and Christians for his knowledge concerning Jewish messianism and the Ten Lost Tribes.

Manasseh ben Israel (1604–1657) had been born to a Marrano family and baptized Manoel Dias Soeiro in Madeira, Portugal. His father escaped the Inquisition and fled to Amsterdam where the family resumed their open Judaism. The young Manasseh was a prodigy. He studied at the Jewish academy (yeshivah), delivered public sermons, wrote his first book, and became a congregational rabbi, all while he was still a teenager.

He established Amsterdam's first Hebrew printing press and published not only codifications and interpretations of Jewish law for Jews, but also many works directed to Christians, who were increasingly interested in understanding Judaism and the Talmud. As a result of these writings, the Christian community developed respect for Manasseh ben Israel as the authoritative contemporary scholar of Judaism. (One measure of his unique status that has come down to us is that Manasseh was immortalized in a 1636 etching by Rembrandt, whom he knew.)

Manasseh shared the Protestants' expectation of the imminence of the Messiah's appearance. He also shared their concern for fulfilling the biblical conditions for that appearance, which included locating the Ten Lost Tribes of Israel. On the basis of rabbinic and historical learning, Manasseh was convinced that the Sambatyon River existed. He even related as evidence several reports that when travelers brought back sand from the Sambatyon River and placed it in an hourglass the sand appeared agitated on weekdays but rested on the Sabbath.

The solution of the Ten Tribes problem came for Manasseh in 1644, when the Tribes were finally located in a plausible, previously unexplored venue—the New World. A Marrano, Antonio de Montezinos (who subsequently became Aaron Levi), returned to Amsterdam from his travels in South America with a fantastic tale of definitely identifying Jewish tribes among the South American Indians. He had located members of the tribes of Reuven and Levi in Spanish New Granada (now Colombia). He reported that the Indians there greeted him by reciting the Shema prayer in Hebrew. They observed basic Jewish ritual practices and they claimed descent from Abraham, Isaac, and Jacob.

Manasseh met with Montezinos and had him swear to the truthfulness of his account. Convinced, the rabbi wrote *The Hope of Israel* in 1650, in which he laid out the case for the South American Indians being the long-sought Lost Tribes, complete with

Manasseh's scientific-historical explanation of how they got there.[29]

Manasseh also used his book to advance his second concern about the messianic era. The Bible promised that the Messiah would gather the Jews from the ends of the earth for the Return. Now that the Ten Tribes had been found, all that remained to prepare for the Messiah was to make certain that there actually were Jews at all the ends of the earth to be gathered. The travels of the exiles during the one and one-half millennia of the Diaspora had pretty much taken care of that, with one glaring exception— there were no Jews in England. Jews had been expelled from England in 1290, and none had been allowed to return. This was especially critical, since from both a Euro-centric point of view and according to standard medieval rabbinic terminology, England could be referred to as the end of the earth.

Fortunately, in the middle of the seventeenth century, England was under the influence of the Puritans, marked by the leadership and ultimately the Protectorate (1653–1658) of Oliver Cromwell. Nowhere in the Christian world did the Jewish messianic cause, and Manasseh ben Israel in particular, enjoy better support than in Puritan England. Suddenly, the Jews had acquired a nation of new best friends, and ones who were as focused as the Jews themselves upon bringing on the Messiah. The answer was obvious to the rabbi—Cromwell had to be convinced to readmit Jews to England in order to satisfy the last condition to the appearance of the Messiah. The most bizarre aspect of this scheme was that it actually worked.

First, Manasseh wrote his book (the English version of which he dedicated to the English Parliament) establishing the messianic implications of locating the Lost Tribes in South America. Then, he engaged in extensive correspondence with English clergy about requiring the presence of Jews in England as a condition to the Messiah's appearance. Finally, in 1655, Manasseh ben Israel went to England and presented a petition to Cromwell for readmission of the Jews. Although this first petition was not formally granted, Cromwell did grant a later petition to authorize the construction of a synagogue and the establishment of a cemetery for the Jews, thereby effectively accomplishing Manasseh's goal of readmitting the Jews.[30] Apparently, Manasseh ben Israel's success was a personal one, too. The rabbi from Amsterdam so impressed the ruler of England that Cromwell awarded him a state pension of one hundred pounds per year. Unfortunately, Manasseh ben Israel died soon after, in 1657, upon his return to Amsterdam.

Antonio de Montezinos continued to insist that he was telling the truth about finding the Lost Tribes, even to his deathbed, but no one else was ever able to locate his Jewish Indians.

The seventeenth century's excitement over the Lost Tribes did not end with the story of Jewish tribes in South America. In 1665 a fresh report came from Tunis that the annual caravan to Morocco was not leaving because the Lost Tribes were attacking Morocco. The army was dressed in blue and led by a rabbi and commanders who spoke Hebrew. Although the warriors had no guns, their swords and arrows had been sufficient for the capture of several cities, where they had killed all the inhabitants.

The story gained impetus with retelling. Subsequent versions relocated the attack from North Africa to Arabia and changed the besieged city from Morocco to Mecca. Soon all Europe was full of exciting news about the attack on Mecca. It was clear that God was on the side of the Ten Tribes. Successive reports detailed how the Turks' weapons were ineffective against the Jews, buildings were destroyed by magic, and Mecca had fallen. Europe heard how the Turks had sued for peace at the price of massive land grants to the Jews, and over a million members of the Lost Tribes were finally on the move, coming to settle in these new lands. A universal mood of messianic expectancy seemed to have spread over the world. The next Jewish Messiah answered it beyond anyone's expectations.

Chapter 17

THE GREATEST MESSIAH: BEGINNINGS

Shabbatai found in the Holy Land what he finally needed to make him the greatest—and the worst—of the Jewish Messiahs.

A MONG ALL the Jewish Messiahs since Jesus, it is easy to award titles for the greatest in many categories: the most important historical figure, the most complex character, the largest movement, the most durable following, and the most damaging to the Jewish people. All of these titles would go to the same Messiah, Shabbatai Zevi (1626–1676).[31]

Shabbatai Zevi was born in Smyrna (Ismir), Turkey, on the ninth of Av, 1626. Even the simple date of Shabbatai Zevi's birth resounds with messianic echoes. In the Jewish calendar, the ninth day of the month of Av is perpetually commemorated as the day of triple tragedy for the early Jewish nation. According to tradition, the First Temple (586 BCE), the Second Temple (70 CE), and the Betar fortress of Bar Kokhba's revolt (135 CE) all fell to siege on the ninth of Av. Jewish legend has it that, as a sort of compensation, the ninth of Av is also the birthdate of the Messiah. Because the ninth of Av in 1626 (5386 in the Jewish calendar) fell on a Saturday (Shabbat), Shabbatai's parents followed a local custom and named him after the day of his birth.

Shabbatai's heritage was probably Ashkenazi. His father, Mordechei, had started as an egg dealer but advanced himself to become a successful and recognized member of the Jewish community as a broker and agent for English merchants. Shabbatai received a rabbinic education and studied Torah, Talmud and Kabbalah. Unlike some other Messiah figures, he was no prodigy. Indeed, it was not the intellectual workings of his mind that started Shabbatai's career as Messiah, but rather the opposite—a kind of mental breakdown that would reappear throughout the rest of his life.

When he was fifteen, Shabbatai suddenly withdrew from his formal education and became a recluse, immersing himself in solitary Kabbalah study. He embarked upon an ascetic life but struggled to control his sexual urges (which may have reflected normal adolescent issues, or may have been related to his unusually close relationship with his mother, Clara). After about six years of this life, Shabbatai began to develop a group of followers who studied Kabbalah under him. It was at about this time, when he was twenty-one or twenty-two, that Shabbatai had his first mental episode.

Applying today's diagnostic standards to the record of his entire life, Shabbatai fits rather easily into the category of bipolar affective disorder (formerly called manic-depressive).[32] Although not yet apparent in 1648, the rest of Shabbatai's life would be openly marked by alternating periods of manic high states, depressive lows, and apparent normalcy. The manic phase of bipolar disorder often involves grandiose delusions involving a special relationship to God. When Shabbatai started off with his first manic episode, it began with a single word—he pronounced the unpronounceable name of God.

As a matter of linguistics, the biblical Hebrew four-letter word for the name of God (YHVH, referred to as the Tetragrammaton) is unpronounceable because we no longer know the vowel sounds associated with it. The Torah was originally written without vowels, so there is nothing authentic for Jews in the current Christian pronunciation of the name as "Jehovah" or "Yahweh." But the true significance of Shabbatai's act of pronouncing the unpronouncable name was not linguistic, but theological. Jewish ritual law forbids pronouncing the name of God because, since the time of the destruction of the Temple, that name is not to be used until the Messiah has come. When Shabbatai Zevi began to utter the name of God in public, he was doing far more than merely defying custom and propriety. He was in effect making his first claim to be the Messiah.

Throughout his life, Shabbatai would engage in various strange acts in his manic episodes. His first episodes set the pattern. He claimed that he had levitated himself, but that his followers could not see this because they were not sufficiently pure. When his followers noticed that he had a sweet smell, he denied using perfume and insisted that the Patriarchs had visited and anointed him with sweet-smelling oil. (Later versions of his history changed to specify that Elijah, the advance messenger of the Messiah, had performed his anointment.) Also at about this time Shabbatai entered into his first two marriages, each of which ended in divorce on the grounds of his unwillingness or inability to consummate.

As his claim to be the Messiah grew more explicit, Shabbatai moved on from speaking the name of God to performing and advocating other modifications and violations of traditional Jewish law. He led his followers in ritual immersion, but rather than the traditional mikvah bath, he bathed in the sea. He changed the holiday celebrations and violated the dietary prohibitions. He spoke of esoteric spiritual revelations that he had received, and described his uniquely close personal relationship with God. All of this followed from his declaration that the usual rules were inapplicable to messianic times.

To the ordinary Jews of Smyrna, Shabbatai was acting very strangely at least, and perhaps was mad. To the rabbis of Smyrna, Shabbatai Zevi was broadcasting dangerous heresy. In 1651 they excommunicated and banished him. An important part of what made the rabbis so fear him at this early stage of his career was that the Jewish world had once again erupted into an excited state of readiness for the Messiah's appearance.

The year 1648 marked a convergence of several forces pushing the Jews to expect the Messiah. The ground had been prepared by the broad spread of Lurianic Kabbalah. Isaac Luria's sophisticated philosophy actually spoke little about the individual Messiah and instead emphasized the need for universal Jewish participation in fulfilling the commandments in order to bring about the messianic era. This distinction was lost on the succeeding generations of ordinary Jews, leaving Luria's general focus on the messianic era to rekindle the people's hopes for a Messiah during their lifetime.

Tragically, 1648 also amply satisfied the popularly accepted prophesy that the Messiah's appearance would be preceded by suffering for the Jews. Established Jewish communities had previously endured bloody riots led by anti-Semitic demagogues (Fettmilch in Frankfurt am Main in 1614, and Chemnitz in Worms in 1615). Then in 1648, the Chmielnicki massacres raged through Poland, killing tens of thousands of Jews. Surely if God were going to send a Messiah, it seemed to be the right time for it.

Finally, along with the Jewish people's intense suffering and peril came that other mainstay of Jewish messianic expectation— calculations. Since the Hebrew language uses letters of the alphabet to express numbers, every number has an equivalent word or abbreviation associated with it. In the Hebrew calendar, the year 1648 was counted as 5408, and some declared that its corresponding letters could be read as referring to the period of the End of Days.

In short, by 1648 the Jews were acutely ready for their Messiah. All that they needed was a satisfactory candidate—someone who was able to believe in himself, inspire others to follow, impress the people with mystical messianic utterances, and work miracles. The young Shabbatai Zevi was definitely a contender, but he needed more if he were to win the crown. It would take him fifteen additional years of travels, adventures, and controversy before he would meet his destiny and become recognized by much of the Jewish world as the Messiah.

After Shabbatai's expulsion from Smyrna, he wandered through Greece and Turkey, but his most important stop was in Salonika (now Thessaloniki). His stay there ended with the excesses of another of his manic phases. His increasingly wild messianic claims led to a bizarre marriage ceremony. Shabbatai summoned the shocked rabbis of Salonika to the synagogue where he stood under the traditional wedding canopy (chuppa) with a Torah, and asserted that he was now married to the Torah.

The outraged rabbis of Salonika likewise banished Shabbatai, and he continued his wanderings in 1658, travelling in Constantinople, Smyrna again, Rhodes, and Cairo. Along the way he continued his alternating cycles of depression, normalcy, and ecstatic episodes of strange acts. During the latter periods, he further infuriated the rabbis and suffered more community expulsions, excommunication, and even a forty-stroke lashing for his extraordinary statements and actions.

He declared that the coming of the messianic era meant that the biblical commandments were no longer binding. He celebrated the three annual Jewish festivals (Succoth, Pesach [Passover], and Shavuoth) in a single week. He dressed a large fish in baby clothes and displayed it in a carriage to announce the beginning of the messianic era (which, according to legend, would begin under the sign of Pisces). He proclaimed that God now permitted everything.

Then, in what appears to have been an effort to gain control over his raging emotional cycles, Shabbatai Zevi moved to Jerusalem in 1662, hoping to live a quiet, reclusive life of study, fasting, and solitude. For a little while, at least, Shabbatai did manage to maintain a relatively low profile in Jerusalem. The rabbis there apparently excused his occasional periods of wildness, and were impressed with his ascetic devotion to study. They sent Shabbatai to Egypt as an emissary of the Palestine Jewish community in 1663. His year in Cairo was marked by more study, more emotional fluctuations, and his "fourth" and strangest marriage.

What marriage could surpass in strangeness Shabbatai's scandalous first two marriages, which he could not or would not consummate, and his blasphemous third "marriage" to the Torah? It would take a very special bride, and Shabbatai found her. His third wife, Sarah, had a background and reputation almost as unique as Shabbatai's. She was a Polish Jew whose parents had been killed in the 1648 pogroms when she was a young child. She was raised by a Polish Catholic family and worked in a convent. She then progressed to a career for which training in a convent is not a typical prerequisite.

Sarah lived a notoriously immoral life in Amsterdam, Mantua, and Leghorn. The community regarded her as a prostitute or perhaps a madwoman. She practiced fortune telling and was impressed with her own childhood dreams foretelling that she would become the bride of the Messiah. As the reputation of Shabbatai Zevi spread, Sarah heard voices telling her that he was the Messiah whom she was destined to marry. She came, or was brought by Shabbatai, to Cairo, where they were married on March 31, 1664. Once again Shabbatai announced that he was postponing physical consummation of the marriage, this time to await the divinely appointed moment. Meanwhile he prepared for that moment by declaring a new doctrine—upon her marriage to him, Sarah had been reborn a virgin. (At a banquet the following year in Smyrna, Shabbatai announced that he would finally initiate relations with his bride that night. To satisfy any skeptics, the next morning he publicly displayed the stained nuptial bedsheets.)

As many have learned, marriage does not always cure everything. Things did not go well for Shabbatai Zevi. He fell into another of his deep, soul-distressing depressions. Once again the answer seemed to be to go to Palestine, but this time not for quiet study. Shabbatai had heard about a bright rabbinical student who had the remarkable power to read people's souls and cure their troubles. The wounded Messiah therefore returned to Palestine, not to further his ministry, but to seek desperately needed help. Better than the cure he sought, Shabbatai found in the Holy Land what he finally needed to make him the greatest—and the worst—of the Jewish Messiahs.

Chapter 18

THE WORLD DISCOVERS THE MESSIAH

It has been estimated that over a million Jews believed in Shabbatai Zevi the Messiah, at a time when this constituted as much as 50% of total world Jewry.

WHAT SHABBATAI Zevi found in Palestine in 1665 was Abraham Nathan ben Elisha Hayyim Askenazi (1643–1680), called "Nathan of Gaza." And if a depressed Shabbatai had sought out Nathan in order to be changed, he certainly got what he came for, and more. For Nathan had dreamed his own vision, and in it God showed him the face of the Messiah. It was the face of Shabbatai Zevi.

It is a measure of the depth of Shabbatai's depression at this point that he could not at first accept this confirmation of his status as Messiah. Only after weeks of their traveling and talking together could Nathan convince Shabbatai that he really was the Messiah. From that point on, Nathan of Gaza became the principal biographer, official theologian, personal secretary, business manager, public relations genius, and inspired advocate for the Messiah Shabbatai Zevi. It was an awesome partnership.

On the festival of Shavuoth, 1665, Nathan announced (some say, uttered in a trance) to the rabbis who had gathered in Gaza for the traditional night of study that Shabbatai Zevi was the Messiah. On May 31, 1665, Shabbatai acknowledged what Nathan had declared—Shabbatai was the Messiah. Word of these announcements spread rapidly throughout Palestine and the rest of the Jewish world. Judaism would never be the same.

It is difficult today to imagine how the entire seventeenth century worldwide Jewish community could have become so inflamed with Shabbatai fever in such a brief time. The primary element appears to have been the miracles. According to the official theology that Nathan soon developed for the movement, Shabbatai did not have to work any miracles. His followers were expected to accept him on faith. Still, the people had been taught to expect miracles from a Messiah, and in the months following Nathan's and Shabbatai's announcements the people were not disappointed. Shabbatai Zevi became a fountain of miracles. Jews throughout Europe and the Middle East eagerly awaited the next miracle story recounted in correspondence sent to their communities from Nathan of Gaza, or through a merchant or traveler, or in a letter from some contact in Smyrna (the community that had now became headquarters for Shabbatai and his growing entourage).

Suddenly Shabbatai Zevi was regularly performing miracles in public. He correctly predicted the sudden deaths of several individuals. He correctly predicted a day of darkness and hailstones. He had a fire set in a public square and walked through it several times. And of course there was Elijah, traditional advance messenger of the Messiah. At first the world was excited to hear that Elijah had appeared in the Aleppo (Syria) synagogue and magically filled the charity box. Soon Elijah sightings became rather commonplace, especially in Smyrna. He was seen often as a beggar in the street, and, although he apparently preferred invisibility when attending formal functions, guests at Smyrna banquets and celebrations were certain that they felt his presence.

Even the spirit of the most revered predecessor Messiah, Shlomo Molkho, was enlisted to further Shabbatai's cause. The Pinkas Synagogue in Prague possessed several relics of Shlomo Molkho's clothing and banners, and they were displayed periodically, except for one. The synagogue had stopped showing a small yellow silk-fringed garment (presumably what is called a talit katan) embroidered with unreadable inscriptions, because looking at the symbols caused blindness. Now Shabbatai declared that the garment could be viewed. When the elders of the synagogue examined it, the previously incomprehensible symbols had been magically rearranged to declare that Shabbatai Zevi would become the Messiah in the year 5426 (1666).

By now the rabbis of Smyrna felt powerless to resist the Messiah and his adoring followers. Shabbatai had, in fact, become the center of the city's religious authority, and he acted the part. He moved about the city in regal splendor, bearing a scepter and wearing a trailing robe carried by two rabbis. These last attendants certainly seem to have been an unnecessary extravagance, since he also had carpets rolled out on the streets before him as he walked through the city. All of this pomp established a self-feeding cycle, so that news of Shabbatai's royal style increased worldwide belief in him, while the increased belief and support emboldened him to act out more extravagant gestures.

Shabbatai Zevi's reign in Smyrna reached a frenzied climax in December of 1665. The Bible says that when the Messiah finally appears, common men and women will be given the gift of prophecy. Suddenly mass prophecy broke out like a contagious disease in Smyrna, as well as in Allepo, Damascus, and Safed. The phenomenon was observed and reported by religious leaders, travelers, and officials, many of whom were not followers of Shabbatai and some of whom were not even Jewish. Hundreds of men, women, and children (as young as four), most of whom could not speak Hebrew, fell down in convulsions and spoke from their trances in Hebrew, quoting phrases from the Bible and the Zohar. They declared that Shabbatai Zevi was God's true Messiah, and that he would soon lead the Return of the Jews to the Holy Land. Riding the crest of this ecstatic wave, Shabbatai took his final actions in Smyrna that showed the world he was worthy of all this adulation.

On the Sabbath of December 12, 1665, Shabbatai went to the Portuguese Synagogue, the center of his remaining opposition in the city. The frightened congregation had barred the door, but Shabbatai broke down the door with an ax, and took over the services. He declared that the congregation was exempt from the obligation to pray, and made them pronounce the name of God. He preached wildly and blasphemously. He took a Torah scroll in his arms and serenaded it with an old Castilian love song ("Meliselda, the Emperor's Daughter"). Shabbatai concluded this most bizarre service by awarding some of his loyal followers with sovereignty over various kingdoms throughout the world, to be effective as soon as he had completed the Restoration.

On the following Monday, December 14, 1665, Shabbatai Zevi formally proclaimed that he was the Messiah, and as fitting for such a momentous day, he also declared that the Monday of proclamation was a Sabbath. Then he finally made the announcement for which the Jewish community had been waiting for 1,600 years—he would begin the Redemption on the fifteenth day of the month of Sivan, 5426 (June 18, 1666).

The reaction of world Jewry to all this was staggering. It has been estimated that over a million Jews believed in Shabbatai Zevi the Messiah, at a time when this constituted as much as 50% of total world Jewry. The printing presses of London, Hamburg,

Amsterdam, and Venice struggled to keep up with the news. There were skeptics, of course, but even respected rabbis who opposed the movement felt they had to keep their silence in the face of the vehemence of Messiah's supporters. Both the common people and the most educated and wealthy believed. This was not a movement born only of personal suffering. Support was also strong in affluent Jewish communities free of harsh discrimination. In Amsterdam, several millionaires pledged to give all their wealth to Shabbatai.

The movement also overrode the normal distinctions between Sephardi and Ashkenazi Jews. Support was strong in communities settled by former Conversos and Marranos who had fled the Inquisition or suffered expulsion from Spain and Portugal, but it was also strong in the Polish and Russian communities that had survived the pogroms. Although Shabbatai Zevi naturally exerted a strong influence in the largely Sephardi communities in the Middle East where he lived, he also had strong connections to the Ashkenazi Jews in distant Europe. Both his wife, Sarah, and his chief supporter, Nathan of Gaza, were Ashkenazi. Nathan aggressively reached out to the Ashkenazi community by promising them that the sole bloodshed permitted in the otherwise complete peace of the messianic era would be in retribution for the 1648 pogroms.

In addition, Shabbatai appealed to the Ashkenazi community when he satisfied the theological requirement for two Messiahs by asserting that he was the second, successful Messiah of the House of David. For the initial, failed military Messiah of the House of Joseph, Shabbatai named an unknown Polish Jew, a Rabbi Abraham Zalman, whom he claimed had been killed while opposing the Chmielnicki pogroms.

Shabbatai Zevi's movement transcended national divisions as well as those of social class and religious-cultural heritage. This was a truly international phenomenon, including followers from Turkey, Palestine, Egypt, Morocco, Italy, Germany, Austria-

Hungary, Poland, Russia, the Balkans, Central Europe, Holland, France and England. Although this spread was impressive, the most astounding feature of the movement was not its breadth, but its depth.

When the first letters describing the Messiah and his miracles arrived in these distant countries, they were often brought to the local synagogue and read to the congregation. Even these initial reports were often enough for people to abandon their businesses and sell or give away all their property, so as to be ready for the Redemption. Synagogue services throughout the world were changed to include a specific prayer for Shabbatai Zevi, the Messiah King. Publishers printed new prayer books written by Nathan of Gaza, featuring a picture of the new Messiah.

Jews sold their assets to non-Jews for whatever they could get. In cities where Jews were important in commerce, business stopped. English merchants dealing in Smyrna had to get Shabbatai to issue a letter threatening that any of his followers who continued to ignore their trade debts would not be allowed to accompany him in the Redemption.

In many cities Jews held celebrations, banquets, and festive public processions in honor of the Messiah's coming. With the Redemption expected so soon, Jews were no longer concerned about giving offence to their neighbors or to the civil authorities. Along with the celebration came prayer, study, and rituals of purification. Jews practiced immersion in cold seawater, lying naked in the snow, public self-flagellation, and other mortifications. Fasting became dangerously popular, especially continuous fasts lasting three or even six days. Constantinople, Ferrara, and other cities reported deaths from over-zealous fasting.

Some Jewish communities paid special attention to the statement in the Talmud that the Messiah would appear only when all of the unborn souls of the world had been born. To expedite any necessary remaining births, the Salonika Jewish community arranged for the marriages of their young children, aged ten to twelve, in mass ceremonies of several hundred couples at a time. Throughout Europe, wealthy young Jewish men married Jewish orphan girls who had no dowries.

Jews were also concerned about the logistics of the Return. The applicable assumptions were often geographically determined. Jewish communities in coastal, seafaring nations naturally presumed that when the Messiah summoned them, they would travel to Palestine by ship. Communities in Holland jointly sold their assets to be ready to sail. Expensive homes were sold at a fraction of their value. Since the Dutch and English were formally at war, one group of Dutch Jews filed in advance a formal petition (February 5, 1666) with the King of England requesting exemption from seizure for the ship that they were certain would be sailing soon. Even the Inquisition was prepared for the ocean traffic. The Supreme Council of the Spanish Inquisition ordered the arrest of any Conversos trying to sail to Palestine to join in the Redemption.

Jews in non-maritime communities had to contemplate alternative transportation. Clouds were especially popular. Many Jews in Russia, Poland, Germany, Greece and Turkey believed that they would be traveling to the Holy Land on a cloud. This certainly provided a logical answer for infants, pregnant women, and the infirm. Some Jewish communities in these countries were so certain of the imminence of their flight that they would begin to celebrate whenever they saw an approaching cloud. A Jew in Greece fell to his death when he tried to hasten the Redemption by leaping to a cloud from his rooftop.

Each community generally expressed its fervor in its own way, perhaps demonstrating cultural differences. In Venice, some Jews were so certain they would soon be transported to the Holy Land that they dug up the bones from their ancestors' graves so they could bring them along.

In Amsterdam, the community had to add seating at the

synagogues and the academies (yeshivot) where Jews suddenly crowded for prayer and study. Wealthy Amsterdam Jews redirected their funds from the gambling houses to synagogue charity.

Gambling remained a little dearer to the hearts of the English. In his entry for the third week of February, 1666, the diarist Samuel Pepys (1633-1703) recorded that Jews in London were expressing the ultimate theological confidence: they were giving ten-to-one odds that, within two years, Shabbatai Zevi would be recognized by the entire world as the true Messiah King. London's Jewish bookmakers accepted wagers of more than ten thousand pounds on this basis. The same odds had previously been offered by the Sephardi Jews of Hamburg until the leaders of that Jewish community banned such wagering.

The Christian world took note of the Jews' excitement. London witnessed a wave of reconversions to Judaism by New Christian merchants—many of whose families had become Christians in order to live in England when Jews were barred—who were now anxious not to miss out on participating in the Redemption. Even in Boston, the sermons of Increase Mather applauded the many reports that the Ten Tribes were approaching Jerusalem, signaling the imminence of the Messiah.

In Vienna, Jews followed the Amsterdam pattern. They adopted new prayer books established by Nathan of Gaza, featuring prayers for Shabbatai Zevi as Messiah King. They ignored business to pray and engage in penance and self-mortification. Some Viennese Jews, their messianic fervor somewhat cooled by their sense of civic loyalty and orderliness, formally requested the Emperor's advance permission to emigrate to Palestine.

In Hamburg, Shabbatai Zevi may not have worked an actual miracle, but he certainly achieved a unique accomplishment—in order to hear the latest letters from Smyrna relating the Messiah's progress, Ashkenazi Jews attended the Sephardi Portuguese synagogue. The news was so heartening that one Hamburg synagogue dropped plans to send a delegation to Shabbatai Zevi because by the time the delegation could arrive, Shabbatai would doubtless be sitting on his throne in Jerusalem. The synagogues in Hamburg were not large enough for the crowds, so prosperous merchants established new institutions where they went three times daily to pray, give charity, practice penance and mortification, and generally prepare for the messianic era.

The Jews of Hamburg were so confident about Shabbatai Zevi that a legal document between two synagogue congregations fixing the payment terms for cemetery property rights included a special "Messiah clause." If the Redemption occurred before the second installment payment was due, the money would instead be donated for the rebuilding of the Temple in Jerusalem.

It is not surprising that all this Jewish excitement in the presence of their Christian or Muslim neighbors generated some serious conflicts with the governments and populations where the Jews lived. In Poland, Jewish enthusiasm over Shabbatai was so open and universal that many anti-Semitic riots broke out. To restore public order King Jan Casimir banned the display or possession of Shabbatai Zevi's portrait or any pamphlets or notices mentioning him.

In Persia some Jews abandoned their farms and lived in the fields, awaiting the Return. When the local governor became concerned that they would not be able to pay taxes if they did not work, the Jews pledged to pay a penalty if the Messiah did not come and begin the messianic era within the next three months. (The Jewish community eventually paid the agreed penalty.)

An opposite economic reaction occurred in several German states and principalities. There, Christian debtors refused to repay their trade debts to the Jews, since the Jews kept insisting that they would be leaving soon. The Jews then turned to the civil governments for protection, pointing out that if they couldn't collect their debts, they wouldn't be able to pay their taxes. This got the attention of the ruling authorities, which passed laws protecting the Jews against riots and directed local officials to help the Jews collect their debts from defaulting Christians.

Worldwide excitement reached the boiling point in early 1666. The Jews expected Shabbatai Zevi to begin the Restoration immediately. Shabbatai did not disappoint them. Finally, the word went out to all Jewish communities: Shabbatai was on the move. His first step to become the Messiah King in Jerusalem was a logical one. It was announced that Shabbatai had set out for Constantinople (Istanbul) to receive the Sultan's crown of dominion over Palestine and all the other lands of the Turks. The story was almost correct.

Chapter 19

THE DISGRACE OF THE MESSIAH

According to the common vision, Shabbatai would next reach out and seize the Sultan's crown. Instead, Shabbatai was given an immediate choice: He must either suffer torture and death, or convert to Islam.

JUST AS the reports promised, in early 1666 Shabbatai Zevi left for Constantinople to depose the Sultan, Mehemed IV. There were also widespread stories that a huge army of the Ten Lost Tribes was already on the move in Arabia. Nathan of Gaza had predicted that Shabbatai would seize the crown from the Sultan with the help of God alone, not an army. Thus the only uncertainty among the world's ecstatic Jews was whether the Sultan would grant the crown freely or lose it through a holy battle. The end, they were certain, was ordained.

Perhaps it was. But the end turned out to be a shameful disaster that even Shabbatai's harshest opponents never envisioned. For Shabbatai Zevi finally accepted from the Sultan not a crown, but a turban.

The disgrace did not happen immediately. The Sultan's Grand Vizier, Ahmed Koprulu, stopped Shabbatai's ship at sea and arrested the Jewish Messiah. Although Shabbatai was originally imprisoned in Constantinople, he was soon moved to the fortress of Abydos, in Gallipoli, where he began one of history's strangest imprisonments. The fortress was normally used for holding persons of high rank awaiting trial, so its conditions were far above what we think of as a prison. On top of this, through enormous bribes paid by his followers Shabbatai Zevi was able to turn his already comfortable prison into an extravagant palace.

The Messiah held court there in the most opulent fashion. In a large chamber furnished with fine furniture and rugs, Shabbatai sat robed in royal splendor and received thousands of visitors and delegations from Persia, Italy, Poland, Germany, France, Holland, and other Jewish communities throughout the world. Those communities that couldn't afford to send their own delegations would eagerly seek letters from the many rabbis who were visiting or staying in Gallipoli.

Visitors found Shabbatai dressed in red, holding a golden staff and a silver fan, and sitting next to a Torah scroll also covered in red. The chamber walls were draped with golden carpets, and the floor was covered with rugs woven of gold and silver. The Messiah's table was made of silver with gold and jewels, and he ate from gold and silver vessels studded with jewels. Shabbatai's wealthy visitors supplied all of this; they also bribed the guards to permit their visits. Some visitors came daily, while others even bribed their way into staying at the prison so that they could be part of the Messiah's regular court.

There were new miracle stories. Many people saw a pillar of fire and stars above the fortress. Assassins sent by the Grand Vizier to kill Shabbatai mysteriously fell dead in the Messiah's presence. Even the phenomenon of mass prophecy recurred, involving many people over several months in Constantinople and Egypt.

As word reached the world Jewish community of how lavishly Shabbatai reigned among the Turks, the fact that he was in prison seemed to lose all significance. Using a term from the Psalms, the Messiah and his followers called the fortress his "Tower of Strength." The evidence of his continued power despite imprisonment confirmed the people's belief in him. The fact that the Turks allowed Shabbatai to live like an Oriental potentate signaled that he would soon be recognized as the temporal ruler of that part of the world. His following grew. There were so many thousands of Jews who came to be near their Messiah in 1666 that traffic at Gallipoli became congested and food prices in Constantinople inflated.

Through all of this, Shabbatai and Nathan continued to issue proclamations of the theological changes wrought by the coming of the messianic age. Shabbatai's new prayer was "Praised be He who permits the forbidden." Since all things would be permitted in the age of the Messiah, Shabbatai and Nathan now declared many of the old restrictions of the Torah no longer applicable. Shabbatai abolished the laws concerning sexual relationships, eating the sinew of the thigh, and the fast on the ninth of Av. He eventually declared that all of the thirty-six major biblical sins were now permitted and even instructed some of his followers that it was their duty to perform such sins in order to hasten the Redemption. Shabbatai himself was served by a group of maidens, often the daughters of prominent supporters, and rumors circulated about his sexual profligacy. He had come a long way from the young man in Smyrna who failed to consummate his first two marriages.

The most thrilling proclamation that issued from Gallipoli was simply a date. Shabbatai Zevi finally proclaimed from his Tower of Strength that the Redemption would begin in the next Jewish year of 5427, which would start in September 1666. He almost got it right. After all, what actually did happen in September 1666 was almost as incredible an event as the Redemption itself would have been.

It began, as did so many important things in Shabbatai's life, with a bizarre situation. A certain Rabbi Nehemiah Kohen had been travelling around Poland making strange prophecies and declarations. Nehemiah may have only been a madman, but Shabbatai Zevi could not ignore one of Nehemiah's obsessions. Nehemiah claimed that he, not the deceased Abraham Zalman named by Shabbatai, was the Messiah of the House of Joseph. This was more than a mere turf war. According to the tradition as already confirmed by Shabbatai, the Messiah of the House of Joseph had to die in battle before Shabbatai, as Messiah of the House of David, could begin the Redemption. But Nehemiah was still alive, so if he was correct then Shabbatai could not be ready to begin the Redemption.

Nehemiah came to the prison at the beginning of September, and the two Messiahs debated Kabbalah non-stop for three days. Neither Shabbatai nor Nehemiah would budge from his claims, but both of them could not be correct. Nehemiah solved the impasse. He went to the Sultan's forces, converted to Islam as a show of reliability, and declared that Shabbatai was a fraud. When added to the Sultan's concerns about reports of sexual promiscuity in the prison and the ever-increasing strength of Shabbatai's followers, the accusation by Nehemiah appears to have been the final straw.

Shabbatai Zevi was suddenly removed from his splendor in Gallipoli and taken to Adrianople (Edirne). On September 16, 1666, he appeared before the Sultan's Privy Council. This was the moment (in September 1666, as predicted by Shabbatai) that his followers had visualized so often over the past year. According to the common vision, Shabbatai would next reach out and seize the Sultan's crown. Instead, Shabbatai was given an immediate choice: He must either suffer torture and death, or convert to Islam.

The Messiah chose conversion. Shabbatai Zevi became Aziz Mehemed Effendi. He was appointed Keeper of the Palace Gates and granted a royal pension. His wife, Sarah, also converted and became the Lady Fatima. In place of the expected crown, Shabbatai had accepted a turban.

The immediate reaction of his followers was what one might expect. After the shock came disbelief. Initially, his followers were united in confidence that the report could not be true. Something else must be happening. Some said that it was all a misunderstanding. An observer must have misconstrued what had really been the ceremony when the Sultan welcomed, or perhaps even crowned, Shabbatai. Some said that it was just a clever trick of Shabbatai to get inside the Turkish government so as to overthrow it. Some acknowledged that perhaps the image of Shabbatai had converted, but insisted that his soul had risen to heaven and escaped.

Nathan of Gaza was unfazed. As always, he provided a theological explanation for the event. Borrowing from the popular doctrines of Lurianic Kabbalah, Nathan explained that this was all part of God's plan. In order to bring on the Reformation, Shabbatai had descended into the darkness of the Muslim world to gather the scattered fragments of the light of creation hidden there. Important things were often not as they seemed. There was an outward reality and an inner reality. Nathan transformed Shabbateanism into a theology of paradox. Once the followers accepted the concept of paradox, they would be able to continue believing in Shabbatai Zevi.

There was even biblical precedent. Shabbatai had gone to live in the Sultan's palace just as Moses had gone to live in the Pharaoh's palace. The comparison to Moses became a part of the Shabbatai story. Like Moses, Shabbatai's followers saw his face glowing as if on fire, although with Moses, it occurred when Moses had been meeting with God, while with Shabbatai, it happened when he was singing. (Shabbatai enjoyed singing Sabbath hymns, which he sang on weekdays, and common romantic ballads.) Nathan prophesied that Shabbatai would travel across the Sambatyon River to find the Lost Tribes and lead them back, with Moses and Moses' daughter "Rebecca" (whom Shabbatai would marry), to capture Jerusalem. Even Shabbatai Zevi himself may have been convinced by the Moses stories. It is said that shortly before his death he made himself a silver serpent on a staff, like the bronze one Moses had made to protect the Israelites.

Another analogy used was to compare Shabbatai's apostasy with Jesus' crucifixion. Both were paradoxical events that, if understood properly, needn't destroy the people's belief in their Messiah. Shabbatai had set the stage for such a comparison when he signed some correspondence as "the only-begotten and first-born Son of God, Shabbatai Zevi, the Anointed of the God of Jacob and Savior of Israel," or "the first-begotten son of God, Shabbatai Zevi, Messiah and Redeemer of the people of Israel."

Nathan of Gaza also had to repair the now-faulty timetable for beginning the Redemption previously announced by Shabbatai. The new date was Passover (April) of 1667, and when that didn't work, early September of 1667 (the last possible date that could satisfy Shabbatai's promise to begin the Redemption in the Jewish calendar year that had started in September of 1666). When both these dates passed without event, Nathan soldiered on. He continued to predict additional dates in 1668, 1673, 1674, and 1675.

This wasn't enough to hold the movement intact. When the great disgrace happened, rabbis who had been silent during 1665 and 1666 suddenly found their voices and condemned the movement. Rabbis in Turkey forbade all Jews from visiting Shabbatai Zevi in Adrianople, banned even the mention of his name, and ordered all community records of the episode destroyed. Rabbis in Palestine, Egypt, Germany, Holland, Poland, Italy, and Russia also ordered documents destroyed.

The vast majority of the ordinary followers were sick with despair. Many were financially ruined. Most Jews were bitterly ashamed—ashamed of Shabbatai's apostasy, ashamed of their own gullibility, and ashamed of how ridiculous Jews now appeared in the eyes of the rest of the world.

Incredibly, the shameful public apostasy still wasn't the end of Shabbatai Zevi as a Jewish Messiah. An inner circle of his followers accepted the explanations of Nathan of Gaza and continued to believe in Shabbatai the Messiah. Perhaps because the Sultan hoped that Shabbatai would obtain additional converts for Islam, the government encouraged Shabbatai to continue his contacts with Jews. The Turks allowed Shabbatai to receive delegations and visitors as he had in the days of imprisonment, and many came despite the rabbis' ban. Some of his followers emulated him and converted to Islam on their own. From time to time, Shabbatai also ordered some of his followers to convert, which they generally did, believing that they were somehow furthering his messianic plans.

Things got very confused. Sometimes Shabbatai spoke with his visitors as if he were a Jew, discussing Torah and Kabbalah. Sometimes he spoke as if he were a Muslim. These reversals could have been a stratagem for fooling the Sultan's spies, or they could have been the alternating consequences of Shabbatai's bipolar emotional states.

In any event the double game eventually caught up with Shabbatai. While traveling with a group of his converted followers in 1672, he was seen attending services in a synagogue. He was immediately arrested by the Sultan's officers and returned to Adrianople in chains. In January 1673, Shabbatai was formally sentenced to death, but the punishment was reduced to exile. The Messiah was sent to his final home: a fortress in Dulcigno (Ulcinj) in Albania.

His wife Sarah followed him into exile, but died in 1674. The next year, Shabbatai married for the last time. His final wife was Michal (referred to by the followers as Jochobed), the daughter of Rabbi Joseph Filosoff of Salonika, a major supporter of Shabbatai.

Shabbatai Zevi died in Dulcigno at the age of fifty, on September 17, 1676 (Yom Kippur, 5437), ten years after his apostasy.

Just as his conversion had failed to do, even Shabbatai Zevi's death could not write the final chapter of his movement. There had been other Jewish Messiahs before him whose followers had continued to believe for several years, or even several generations. The aftermath to Shabbatai Zevi would surpass them all.

Chapter 20

SHABBATAI'S SECRET MOVEMENT SURVIVES

It would seem that any group of secret Jews comprised of three sects that follow competing theologies and revere competing Messiahs would have little likelihood of longevity. But this group was destined to break all the rules (in every sense of that phrase).

B Y ITS nature, it is difficult to conceive of a Messiah movement as being hereditary. Even if it could be, Shabbatai Zevi did not leave appropriate blood heirs. In 1667 Sarah bore a son, Ishmael, who lived with Sarah and Shabbatai in exile as Shabbatai's son. There may have been some question of paternity, since by the time of Ishmael's birth Sarah had reverted to her promiscuous lifestyle. Then, as Shabbatai had earlier prophesied, Ishmael died in adolescence. An illegitimate son, Abraham, also lived with Shabbatai in exile, but he was never a significant figure for the movement. Thus, there was no descendent of Shabbatai Zevi left to carry on. Who, then, would lead the remnants of his followers (the Believers, or

Ma'aminim) stubbornly keeping the faith after Shabbatai's conversion and death?

Shabbatai Zevi's true heirs became those of his followers who reinterpreted his life, restated his philosophy, founded splinter sects, and sometimes claimed Messiah status as successors—or even reincarnations—of Shabbatai. Nathan of Gaza would have been the obvious successor to lead the movement, but he died soon after Shabbatai, on January 11, 1680. Even without Nathan, plenty of candidates for the role of successor remained.

Abraham Miguel Cardozo (1626–1706) wrote extensively about Shabbatean theology, and eventually announced that he was the Messiah of the House of Joseph. He claimed that Shabbatai's widow, Jochobed, had recognized his leadership and offered to marry him. Cardozo later retracted these claims, but perhaps not convincingly enough. His nephew, Shalom, stabbed him to death in a dispute over leadership of the movement.

Mordechai ben Hayyim of Eisenstadt (c.1630–1706) traveled through Germany and Poland, claiming to be Shabbatai Zevi, returned from the dead. He actually claimed to be an improvement on the original. He said he was the true Messiah of the House of David because he was poor, a messianic requirement which the first Shabbatai had failed. Similarly, Yehuda Leib Prossnitz (1670–1730), an uneducated peddler from Moravia, wandered from city to city and eventually declared himself a Messiah shortly before his death.

Yehoshua Heshel Tzoref (1633–c.1700), an uneducated Lithuanian jeweler, was not so much a Shabbatai successor as a surrogate. He claimed that he was only the Messiah of the House of Joseph, and that his role was to reign until Shabbatai Zevi returned from death. He wrote a large and important work of messianic theology and attracted many followers in Vilna and Cracow.

One of his students, Hayim ben Shlomo, called Hayim Malakh (c.1655–1716), together with Judah Hasid, founded the

Society of the Pious ("Hasidim"), a Shabbatean religious group. They led about 1,500 members on a millennial trip to Palestine in 1699, but the group disintegrated in 1700 when the messianic age failed to begin on schedule and Judah Hasid died. Hayim traveled with a statue of Shabbatai Zevi, and apparently proclaimed himself as a Messiah.

Not all of the Messiah figures who appeared immediately after Shabbatai Zevi were his followers, of course. Moshe Hayim Luzzatto, called the "Ramhal" (1707–1747) was not a Shabbatean, but told his students that Elijah had designated him as the Messiah. He wrote messianic works to replace the Zohar and the Psalms, as well as authoring other important Jewish works.

Nehemiah Hiyya Hayyun (1650–1726) preached a form of divine trinity, and predicted that the Restoration would begin by 1740. He attracted a substantial following in Europe, and created very divisive factional disputes, with cross-accusations of heresy and cross-excommunications. Similar intramural controversies raged within the European rabbinate, centering around heresy accusations by Jacob Emden that Jonathan Eibeschuetz, leading rabbi of Hamburg, was a Shabbatean.

All of these men were only peripheral messianic successors of Shabbatai Zevi. Their movements were relatively modest and short-lived. For the most significant and long-term consequences, we must turn to two of Shabbatai's immediate successors and the amazing secret sect they produced. Afterwards, we will meet the only successor Messiah who rivaled Shabbatai Zevi in terms of bizarre actions, a huge international following, and shameful, disastrous consequences.

Shabbatai's widow, Jochobed, designated the Messiah who came closest to being Shabbatai Zevi's official successor. Jochobed and Shabbatai had no children together. After Shabbatai's death she returned to Salonika and declared that Shabbatai's soul now lived within her brother, Jacob Filosoff (c.1650–1690), called by the followers Jacob Querido (Beloved). With the support of their father, Rabbi Joseph Filosoff, Querido led several hundred families in 1683 and 1686 to convert outwardly to Islam, while establishing a secret, inwardly Shabbatean Jewish society (the Jacobins).

Then the Izmirlis, some of the families who had originally converted to Islam during Shabbatai's lifetime but who remained believers in original Shabbateanism, joined Querido's Jacobins in their crypto-Jewish group. The Izmirlis retained a separate identity because they did not recognize the special messianic leadership status claimed by Querido or—after Querido's death on a pilgrimage to Mecca in 1690—by his son Berechiah (d. 1740).

Two sects should ordinarily be more than enough for any secret society, but nothing associated with Shabbatai Zevi was ordinary. Some of the Izmirlis soon split off into a third sect, the Konyosos, who were followers of Baruchya Russo (d. 1720). In 1716, shortly before his death, the Konyosos declared Russo to be the divine Messiah, the sole successor to and reincarnation of Shabbatai Zevi.

It would seem that any group of secret Jews comprised of three sects that follow competing theologies and revere competing Messiahs would have little likelihood of longevity. But this group was destined to break all the rules (in every sense of that phrase). In the first place, these Muslims who were secret Jews were not entirely secret. It didn't take the Turks long to figure out that these outwardly observant Muslims lived in special enclaves in Salonika and never married outside of their group. Apparently because of this refusal to assimilate the Turks called them the Donmeh, meaning "apostates."

Although Jewish rabbinic authorities had banned Shabbateanism, the Donmeh continued underground contacts with Jews, both locally and in Europe. Locally, the Donmeh consulted the regular rabbis of Salonika to settle their internal disputes in a Jewish religious court and to obtain authoritative

Talmudic rulings on Jewish law. Russo's Konyosos also sent emissaries to secret communities of Shabbateans in Europe as missionaries for their branch of the Donmeh movement. As a result, the general Jewish community knew enough about the existence of the Donmeh to engage in rabbinic disputes over whether the Donmeh were truly Jewish for purposes of marriage, family purity, and conversion laws.

Neither the Turks nor the Jews at first learned the whole truth about the covert religious practices of the Donmeh. Each of the three sects built and maintained a secret synagogue at the center of its neighborhood in Salonika. Members owned clandestine handwritten prayer books from which they recited a Shabbatean liturgy mixed with adaptations of some traditional Jewish prayers. Besides rewriting the prayer book, the Donmeh also rewrote the Ten Commandments. The new Eighteen Commandments of the Donmeh changed some of the original rules (in particular, the prohibition against adultery), and added some new ones, including barring intermarriage with true Muslims.[33] The Donmeh also prohibited intermarriage with non-Donmeh Jews.

The most astounding of the Donmeh secret practices were associated with its most radical sect, Russo's Konyosos. Baruchya Russo had developed an extreme theology asserting that the major laws of the Torah had been reversed with the appearance of himself as the Messiah. What the Torah most emphatically prohibited the Messiah now required. This included reversing the rules against incest and illicit sexual relations.

As a reflection of Shabbatai Zevi's penchant for rearranging the Jewish holidays, the most important holiday in the calendar of the Believers had become a version of Purim, normally a secondary but joyous holiday celebrating the Jews' escape from the treachery of Haman, the Prime Minister of ancient Persia. The Shabbatean Purim had little in common with the conventional holiday. Even in Shabbatai Zevi's lifetime, it was celebrated eight days after the standard Purim, and originally commemorated the miracle of Shabbatai having escaped drowning during one of his early immersions in the sea.

The Konyosos sect of the Donmeh now converted the Shabbatean Purim into an annual orgy, when members exchanged spouses for a ceremony called "extinguishing the lights." The Donmeh justified their Purim orgies, and their regular practice of sharing wives and engaging in other sexual activities, by citing biblical precedents. The general Jewish community finally got the picture. By the end of the eighteenth century, enough rumors and suspicions had reached the rabbis so that all the descendents of the Donmeh were excommunicated from the Jewish community on the presumption of bastardy.

Given all this, how long could such a secret group be expected to survive? The Donmeh managed to continue their isolated, secret double lives for almost three hundred years, into the middle of the twentieth century. During this period they grew from a few hundred families to perhaps ten to fifteen thousand members.

They were not powerless in the general society. Salonika happened to be the center of the "Young Turk" revolution in the beginning of the twentieth century, and some Donmeh members and descendents were important participants. Several ministers in the first Young Turk government were Donmeh descendents, and the Minister of Finance, Djavid Bey, was a descendant of Russo and an active leader of the Konyosos sect.

Indeed, the Donmeh might still continue today as a secret entity if it were not for the consequences of war. Among the territorial realignments imposed by the resolution of the Greco-Turkish War after the end of World War I was the transfer of sovereignty over Salonika from Turkey to Greece. Then, in 1924, the Greeks expelled all Turks from Greek lands in exchange for repatriation of Greeks from Turkish territories. Greek officials were unimpressed when the leaders of the Donmeh broke their tradition of silence and tried to explain that, three centuries of outward appearances notwithstanding, they were really Jews, not Turks.

The forced displacement of the Donmeh to Istanbul and elsewhere marked the end of the group. Some of their previously secret documents fell open to public scrutiny. Their next generation wanted a modern life of college education and cultural assimilation. The movement of Shabbatai Zevi, the Messiah who had almost destroyed Judaism in the mid-seventeenth century, finally ended with the exposure and assimilation of the Donmeh in the middle of the twentieth century.

Chapter 21

THE JEWISH-MUSLIM-
CHRISTIAN MESSIAH

---

*Shabbatai declared that his wife was a virgin; Frank
declared that his daughter was The Virgin.*

B ESIDES QUERIDO and Russo, Shabbatai Zevi also had a third
major heir. Although Jacob Frank (1726–1791) was born
fifty years after the death of Shabbatai Zevi, he deserves to be
regarded as Shabbatai's true successor. It is impossible to learn
their stories without contemplating the comparisons, contrasts,
and connections between the two Messiahs. Shabbatai was an
educated rabbi, the son of a successful business broker. He
founded a major Jewish messianic movement, but converted to
Islam and died as Aziz Mehemed Effendi, in unhappy exile.
Frank was uneducated, the son of an itinerant trader. He
founded a major Jewish messianic movement, converted to
both Islam and Christianity, and died as the Baron Jacob Josef
Frank, in wealth and elegance. Shabbatai declared that his wife
was a virgin; Frank declared that his daughter was The Virgin.

Shabbatai's life reflects the distortions of mental illness; Frank's life reflects the machinations of base opportunism.

Jacob Frank was born Jacob ben Judah, in southern Poland (the portion of Ukraine known as Podolia). He received only the most basic Jewish education. After accompanying his father on trading trips to Turkey, Frank became a trader and guide for other tradesmen. In 1752, Frank married Hannah, the daughter of a Bulgarian merchant. They had three children, a daughter Rachel (later called Eva), and younger sons Josef and Rochus.

The area in Poland where Frank grew up was active with underground Shabbatean groups, and received regular visits from missionaries of the Baruchya Russo sect of the Donmeh. Whether this was the initial source of his association with Shabbateanism, or whether it was an encounter with the Donmeh in Turkey, Frank became involved with the Russo sect by 1753 and began to study their secret doctrines. His charisma and ambition soon marked him as a potential leader for the movement, and he began to claim the status of "The Third"—the third reincarnation of the soul of the Messiah, after Shabbatai Zevi and Baruchya Russo. Jacob Frank referred to himself as "the true Jacob," meaning that just as the biblical Jacob completed the accomplishments of Abraham and Isaac, it was up to Frank to complete the work of his predecessor patriarchs, Shabbatai and Russo. This was the beginning of a trinity theme that Frank would return to and rework inventively throughout his life.

Theologically, Frank was in his way as much of a paradox as Shabbatai had been. Frank took pride in his lack of education, identifying himself as one of the unlearned common people (am haaretz). In the conventional sense, he was not intellectually creative. Much of his philosophy was a repackaging of Kabbalistic, Shabbatean, and Christian ideas. Nevertheless, he was capable of continually modifying and developing the theology of his movement to meet the challenges of changing circumstances.

Although there are a few miracle stories in his life (visions of heaven, being saved from the plague, and an occasional healing), Frank was a Messiah who did not depend on miracles. His magic resided in his immense charisma and ruthless determination.

In 1757 Frank returned to Poland, where the Jewish communities treated him as a traveling dignitary. Because of his years in Turkey, he spoke Ladino and was generally assumed by his fellow-Ashkenazi Polish Jews to be a Turkish Sephardi Jew. He was referred to as a *frenk*, then the Yiddish term for a Sephardi Jew, and he appropriated that term as his family name, "Frank."

He made contact with the secret Shabbatean "Believers" in various towns, and in January 1756 was discovered in Lanskroun (now in the Czech Republic) presiding over a religious sexual orgy of the kind practiced by the Russo sect. Frank escaped imprisonment by convincing the authorities that he was a Turkish subject. He fled to Turkey, where he formally converted to Islam in 1757.

When the rabbinic authorities in Poland responded to the Lanskroun incident by excommunicating Frank and his followers, the Jewish community drove the Frankists out of their homes and took their property. Frank's followers developed a unique counter-strategy to protect themselves against this persecution by the Jewish community. The Frankists sought the protection of the Catholic Church. They asked Bishop Dembrowki to institute a disputation (a public debate on essential theological questions, often used by the Inquisition against Jews).

Frank's followers requested ecclesiastic protection on the grounds that their own beliefs were not Jewish, but rather "anti-Talmudist." In the statement of their theology that they submitted to the bishop, Frank's followers emphasized Frank's trinity theory and belief in the Messiah. They cleverly used wording so ambiguous that the bishop naturally thought that their messianic beliefs referred to Jesus of Nazareth. He didn't suspect that they were really talking about Jacob of Podolia.

Bishop Dembrowki finally forced the local rabbis to defend the disputation in June 1757. On October 17, 1757, the bishop, impressed by how the Frankist theology appeared to be so close to basic Christian beliefs, decided in favor of the Frankists and against the "Talmudists" (the Jewish community). The bishop declared that the "anti-Talmudists" (Frank's followers) were entitled to practice their religion, and ordered that all copies of the Talmud within the diocese be seized and burned. It is not clear what the consequences for Polish Jewry might have been if this campaign had continued, but in November of 1757, just as the Talmud burnings were taking place, Bishop Dembrowki suddenly died.

If Dembrowki had been threatening the Frankists at the time, the bishop's sudden death would no doubt have been seen as a miracle confirming that Jacob Frank was the Messiah. Instead, it was the Jewish community who saw the elimination of their scourge as an act of God. This evidence of divine support emboldened the Jews to resume their hostile actions against Frank's followers.

By this time the Frankists had learned how to use the system, and they mounted a bold defense. They formally petitioned the Polish civil authorities to implement the bishop's ruling. On June 16, 1758, King Augustus III issued an order granting royal protection to the Frankists.

Now under the protection of the crown, Jacob Frank and his followers settled in the town of Iwanie, in Poland. Adoring followers gave huge donations to the movement. Frank purchased a palace, and began to live like a nobleman. Jacob ben Judah, who had renamed himself Jacob Frank, now started calling himself the Baron de Frank.

At Iwanie, Frank began to elaborate on the theology of the movement. He modified his trinity concept to parallel Catholicism's Father, Son, and Holy Spirit. Under Frank's theology the trinity was God, the Messiah (Shabbatai Zevi and his reincarnation, Jacob Frank), and God's spirit (the Shechinah, a Kabbalistic concept of the feminine, spiritual aspect of God).

He also extended the paradoxical teachings of Shabbatai Zevi and Baruchya Russo that the coming of the messianic age had transformed sexual prohibitions of the bible into permissions (Shabbatai) or even obligations (Russo). According to Frank, engaging in sexual orgies now became the means to purify the soul from its sins. Debauchery became therapy. Suiting his actions to his words, Frank appointed twelve "sisters" to be his sexual partners at Iwanie.

In a further appropriation of Christian symbolism, Frank also appointed twelve men as his apostles to help disseminate the new theology. Perhaps Frank felt he needed help because he recognized how difficult it might be to convince even his most ardent followers to take the next step. Shabbatai Zevi had descended into the Sultan's palace. The Donmeh had descended into the world of Islam. Now Jacob Frank planned a similar journey—the Frankists must descend into the world of Christianity. In their present halfway status, they were despised by the Jewish community but not yet accepted by the Christians.

Once again the answer was to be found in the Shabbatean philosophy of paradox, and its distinction between external and internal realities. Frank convinced his followers (some of whom had, like Frank, already converted to Islam when they took refuge in Turkey) that the only way for their special form of Judaism to survive was for them outwardly to become Christians. Following the Donmeh precedent, after conversion they would secretly maintain their true religion, live together in one location, and marry only within the sect.

In February 1759, the Frankists told the Church that they were ready to be baptized. Perhaps as the price of being accepted by the Church, they also offered to engage in a second disputation with rabbinic Jewish authorities. For this second disputation, they promised not only to demonstrate the truth of Christianity over the falsity of Talmudic Judaism, but they would also prove the truth of the "blood libel."

The Polish Church and government had repeatedly raised the blood libel—the monstrous anti-Semitic allegation that Jews periodically killed Christian children to use their blood for the ritual of baking Passover matzoh. The Church would enjoy a very sweet victory, indeed, if it could prove the blood libel in public, especially out of the mouths of these former Jews. As a grand finale to this triumph, the disputation would end with the mass baptism of the Frankists, who had promised to deliver five thousand new Christians from Poland, Moravia, Hungary, and Turkey.

The second disputation was held before Father Mikulski in the Cathedral of Lvov (Lemberg) on July 17, 1759, and continued for several sessions until September 10, 1759. As in the first disputation, the rabbis within the diocese were forced to attend and participate. The debate was a spirited one, and garnered much attention within both the Jewish and Catholic communities. Neither side's arguments were conclusive, so Mikulski withheld his final decision until he could receive additional written arguments from the rabbis.

Meanwhile, the baptisms proceeded. Jacob Frank led the first group converting to Christianity in Lvov on September 17, 1759. Conversions also followed in other cities, with the total numbers probably in the thousands. Frank himself had the special honor of undergoing a second baptism in Warsaw on November 18, 1759. This was a royal ceremony, under which Frank became the godson of the King of Poland. Jacob Frank now became Josef Frank, connected to the royal family. The time of his triumph lasted only a matter of weeks.

Although the Lvov disputation had not yet resulted in a decision on any of the theological arguments, it produced one important consequence. Some priests who had been following the proceedings finally woke up to the warnings of the rabbis that Frankists were not sincere Christians. In December 1759, six Frankists confessed to a priest that it was not Jesus but Jacob Frank who was the living God worshipped by the group. Frank was arrested on February 6, 1760, tried by the ecclesiastic court, and sentenced to permanent exile and imprisonment in the fortress of Czestochowa, in southern Poland.

Jacob Frank had claimed to be the reincarnation of Shabbatai Zevi. Now he got his wish. Just as Shabbatai had been sent to the Gallipoli prison at the height of his power and popularity, Frank now was also sent to prison at the peak of his influence. The analogy was not lost on Frank's followers. Like Abydos prison in Gallipoli, the Czestochowa fortress was used to accommodate nobility awaiting trial. Jacob Frank, twice baptized as a Catholic, godson to the King of Poland, and possessing seemingly limitless wealth, must have seemed as noble as any who came there. His guards treated him as befitted the Baron Jacob Josef Frank.

Although the Church's purpose in exiling Frank was to break his evil influence on his followers—the Church still expected that they would become good Christians in his absence—Frank's intended isolation was not enforced. Within a year, Frankists were visiting him and receiving his instructions to the movement. Within two years, his principal followers moved near the fortress, forming a new community of his believers. They had relatively open access to Frank, and even resumed the movement's religious orgies within the prison. Czestochowa became Frank's "Tower of Strength" just as Gallipoli had been for Shabbatai.

Over the years Frank continued to send messages and instructions from the prison to his followers, keeping their spirits afloat and further developing the theology of the movement. In particular, Czestochowa happened to be in the center of an area of intense Catholic emphasis on the Virgin Mary. Frank's fortress itself was near the Jasna Gora monastery that housed a revered icon of the Virgin Mary, a painting called the Black Madonna. Apparently influenced by this, Frank reworked his previous Trinitarian concept. The Shechinah, which in Jewish Kabbalah represented God's soul and feminine aspect, now became "The Lady" (Gavirah), a concept parallel to the Virgin in Christianity.

Originally, Frank's wife was designated for this role, but when she died in 1770, Frank transferred the title to their daughter, Rachel, who was thereupon called Eva. From then on, Eva was worshipped by the Frankists as The Lady, The Maiden, or The Matronita. Frank had given Judaism its Virgin, and his followers were now to regard her as the third incarnation of the Messiah after Shabbatai Zevi and Jacob Frank.

The Frankists also became involved in international political intrigue, and sent secret emissaries to the Russian government and the Eastern Orthodox Church offering to help in the overthrow of Poland and the Catholic Church. Perhaps as a result, when the Russians occupied Czestochowa under the First Partition of Poland in 1772, Frank was freed by the Russian military. He and his daughter and some followers went to Bruenn, Moravia, where he had relatives.

His followers endowed Frank with great wealth, and he displayed it with princely extravagance in Bruenn. He established a grand court, dressing his followers in elaborate uniforms. Frank gave military training to his retinue and educated the children of the movement to become the future leaders of the society he expected to establish. He impressed everyone of importance in Austria, including the Empress Maria Teresa, who granted him an audience. The Austrian nobility was even more intrigued when Frank circulated the rumor that Eva was really the daughter of Catherine the Great.

By 1786, Frank suffered temporary financial problems, and moved his court to Offenbach, near Frankfurt. There, Frank's money problems were somehow solved, and he resumed presiding over a court even more extravagant than at Bruenn. The source of Frank's immense wealth is not clear. Certainly he had many wealthy and devoted followers who gave him enormous amounts. He also may have used his movement's system of secret messengers and clandestine cells to engage in highly paid espionage assignments for various governments in the constant political turmoil involving Austria-Hungary, Turkey, and the Balkans.

Whatever the sources, his wealth was once again on display in Offenbach. His retinue wore uniforms trimmed with gold and rode fine horses. Frank and his family lived in an opulent palace, very much in the oriental style, sitting on silk cushions and dining on gold plates. Even his death was magnificent. When he died from a stroke in 1791, he was given a lavish funeral attended by many followers as well as the local nobility.

The death of a Messiah is, of course, the ultimate test of the movement. Sometimes the members' disillusionment leads to immediate dissolution of the movement. Often there is some period of momentum carrying a small core of faithful for a generation or two. Jacob Frank thought he had created a secret weapon for perpetuation—his daughter Eva, The Lady. Unfortunately, when a movement depends so much on the personal charisma of the founder, it is difficult even for a designated successor to carry on.

In the beginning, followers came to Eva's residence in Offenbach, called Gottes Haus (God's House), to show their devotion to the woman whom Jacob Frank had declared to be an incarnation of the Messiah, the divine Lady, and a Romanov princess. But Eva was not so much a successor as a relic of Jacob Frank. Financial support gradually dried up. Eva Frank still reigned and was worshipped as the divine Lady, but in continually narrowing circumstances and by a continually shrinking circle of followers. She survived both her younger brothers, and died in 1817. None of Jacob Frank's children left heirs. Eva Frank died a bankrupt, without power or significant followers, leaving as her unique legacy the story of Judaism's only female Messiah.

The Frankist movement itself managed to retain an identity and influence into the second half of the nineteenth century. Frankist families (both those living as Christians and those living as Jews) lived in particular areas in Poland, Hungary, Austria, Germany, Bohemia, and Moravia, and tried to marry only among themselves. Many continued to meet secretly and exchanged clandestine religious writings. In the summers, the German groups regularly held secret meetings in the resort of Carlsbad.

Some very prominent families arose out of these Frankist groups, especially in Warsaw and Prague. It is said that by the middle of the nineteenth century the majority of the lawyers in both these cities were descended from Frankist families. United States Supreme Court Justice Felix Frankfurter is reported to have received a copy of Eva Frank's portrait from his mother, a descendent of a Prague Frankist family.

The primary impression left by Jacob Frank's story is that of an incredibly ambitious, vain, domineering conniver. He was in a sense the most ecumenical Messiah—he ruthlessly manipulated Jews, Shabbateans, Muslims, Catholics, and Russian Orthodox alike. He meddled in political intrigues with Russia, Poland, Austria-Hungary, Turkey and the Balkans. He used the generosity of his followers to elevate his personal life style to ever-increasing opulence and extravagance. Indeed, the course of his movement can be read simply from the progression of his names: From Jacob ben Judah to Jacob Frank, to Josef Frank, to the Baron Jacob Josef Frank.

Most tragically, Jacob Frank pursued his ambitions at terrible costs for the Jewish people. He corrupted a century of followers by ritualizing the lowest forms of sexual licentiousness. He did not even hesitate to appropriate two of the basest anti-Semitic weapons—the disputation and the blood libel—and use them against the Jewish community in order to further his movement. If it were not for the world-wide breadth and depth of the devastating consequences of the Shabbatean movement that preceded him, we would surely name Jacob Frank as Judaism's greatest—and worst—Messiah.[34]

Chapter 22

THE HASIDIC MASTER
AS MESSIAH

While most Hasidic Masters did not claim to be the Messiah and their followers did not regard them as Messiahs, there were some important exceptions.

YOU MIGHT expect that the twin debacles of Shabbatai Zevi and Jacob Frank would finally put an end to Jews' readiness to embrace and deify the next Messiah. On the contrary, not only did these experiences fail to stop Jewish messianism in general, but some observers believe that the next major Jewish movement with messianic aspects was at least a partial aftermath (either as an extension or a reaction) to the disasters of Shabbateanism and Frankism.

Hasidism, a major Jewish movement arising in the eighteenth century, de-emphasized study and focused instead on this-world concerns of the common man. Hasidism embodied its teachings in simple parables and folk-tales rather than lofty intellectual writings. It advocated simple individual and communal joy as a means of drawing close to God.[35] The arguably messianic aspect of Hasidism is found in the role of the individual tzadik (a man of righteousness, commonly referred to as the Master, or rebbe), each of whom was at the center of his particular group of hasidim (disciples or followers). The Hasidic Master was more than a wise and charismatic leader; he was often a mystic who performed miracles and communicated with God. While most Hasidic Masters did not claim to be the Messiah and their followers did not regard them as Messiahs, there were some important exceptions. Of the many eighteenth and nineteenth century Hasidic Masters, four in particular seem to qualify as Messiah figures.

The first is the founder of Hasidism, Israel ben Eliezer, (1700–1760), known as the Ba'al Shem Tov (Master of the Good Name, sometimes called by the acronym the Besht). From humble beginnings in Podolia in Ukraine, the Ba'al Shem Tov developed the concept of close relationship with God through individual joyousness and good deeds. This philosophy was able to be understood and practiced by the common Jew, even under conditions of restricted education, poverty, and the need to work hard to support a family. As a result, the teachings of the Ba'al Shem Tov attracted a large following during his lifetime (perhaps one hundred thousand) that continued to grow under the leadership of his disciples and successors.

The Ba'al Shem Tov left no organized writings, and there is no direct evidence in his disciples' writings that he or his followers expressly claimed that he was the Messiah. Nevertheless, the tales of his life emphasize that hallmark of the Messiah: miracles. He shares with several other Messiahs and biblical figures a story of miracle birth—before his conception, Elijah (forerunner of the Messiah) announced his coming birth to his father. His life, too, was full of the kind of miracle stories found in the Hebrew and Christian Bibles. For example, he triumphed in battles with Satan's werewolf and other sorcerers, healed the sick, talked with animals embodying human spirits, resurrected a bride after her death, and drove out ghosts.

He also told of a vision of ascending to paradise where he learned that the Messiah would only appear when the Ba'al Shem Tov's insights were understood and accepted by the Jewish people. Thus, while it could be argued that he did not fully qualify as a Messiah figure, the Ba'al Shem Tov was revered by his followers as at least a semi-divine miracle-worker. The messianic themes in the lives of some of his successors are beyond debate.

The most significant and open messianic claims for any of the early Hasidic Masters were proclaimed by and for the Ba'al Shem Tov's great-grandson, Rabbi Nachman of Bratslav (1772–1811), who likewise was from Podolia. He taught by means of stories that were sometimes difficult to interpret, but his messianic claims were clear.

He asserted that he was the last of the four great teachers, after Simeon ben Yochai (purported author of the Zohar), Isaac Luria, and the Ba'al Shem Tov. Nachman of Bratslav developed an elegant solution to the traditional requirement for two Messiahs— the failed Messiah of the House of Joseph and the successful Messiah of the House of David—by combining them. He claimed that his soul encompassed the souls of both of the Messiahs. Rabbi Nachman described the true tzadik as the Messiah who will redeem the Jewish people. He regarded himself as a true tzadik.

Unlike general Jewish messianism, Hasidism often passed leadership of a sect from the founding Master to successive generations of his descendents. In this vein, Nachman of Bratslav indicated that if he were not permitted to complete the Redemption, one of his descendents would be the Messiah. Ironically, of all of the early Hasidic Masters, Rabbi Nachman suffered seeing all of his descendents predecease him. Despite this, the force of his message was strong enough somehow to sustain and institutionalize his movement. The Bratslaver sect continues today, a charismatic movement whose messianic leader died almost two centuries ago.

The final two early Hasidic Masters who were messianic figures were not as significant as the Ba'al Shem Tov or Nachman of Bratslav, but their messianic claims were more prominent. Rabbi Israel of Ruzhin (1797–1850) was the great-grandson of the Ba'al Shem Tov's immediate successor, Dov Ber. Israel of Ruzhin claimed that his soul incorporated the soul of the Ba'al Shem Tov. He and his followers also believed that Israel of Ruzhin was the Messiah. Because he had been born to substantial wealth, he broke with the Hasidic tradition of simplicity and disregard for wealth, establishing a lavish court where he presided over his followers. Even the government was concerned with his messianic claims. He was held in a Russian prison for several years on suspicion that he had killed two rivals in a scheme to become King of the Jews.

Rabbi Itzak Eizik of Komarno (1806–1874) was the final early Hasidic Master who asserted Messiah status. He told of his miraculous birth. He declared that his soul included fragments of the souls of many of the great Messiahs and leaders, such as the Ba'al Shem Tov, Hayyim Vital, Isaac Luria, Rabbi Akiba, and Moses. He devoted his life to promoting the task of repair of the world (the Lurianic precondition to the coming of the Messiah) but finally acknowledged that neither his soul nor the age in which he lived was pure enough to permit beginning the messianic era.

Chapter 23

THE MESSIAH WHO RETURNED FROM THE DEAD AND OTHER YEMENITE MESSIAHS

The greatest miracle, of course, was the initial one—
Shukr's resurrection after being beheaded. He even bore
the scar on his neck.

MAIMONIDES' TWELFTH century advice to the Yemenites to abandon their enthusiasm for Messiahs was apparently forgotten by the end of the fifteenth century. A new Messiah arose in southern Yemen in 1495. Little is known about the Messiah of Beyhen except that many of his followers were Muslims who had previously converted from Judaism. He developed a large and well-equipped army whose threatening power convinced the Arab authorities to take action. After the Messiah's troops were defeated by the King of San'a (the modern San'a is now the capital of The Republic of Yemen), the King took punitive action to prevent any recurrence. He killed the entire Jewish community living in that area, and Jews did not return to that part of Yemen for over a hundred years.

Even such a bleak consequence did not deter the Yemenites from continuing their messianic hopes. In the seventeenth century the Yemenite Jewish community was an ardent part of the worldwide support for Shabbatai Zevi. Before Shabbatai's apostasy, most Yemenite rabbis enthusiastically endorsed his claim to be the Messiah. The Yemenite Jews accepted with fervor Shabbatai's promise to begin the Redemption by 1666. They prepared for the impending Redemption as so many other Jewish communities did: stopping their business or work, selling or abandoning their property, and lending or giving away their money. Their reaction was so passionate that even their Muslim neighbors were impressed, and many Muslims became convinced that the Jews' belief in Shabbatai must be warranted.

Shabbatai's arrest not only disappointed the Yemenite Jews, but also subjected them to the angry response of their Muslim neighbors. Widespread pogroms erupted, and the Imam humiliated the Jewish community with a series of punitive laws to demonstrate the Jews' subordination to the Muslims. Jews were forbidden to wear turbans, drink wine on Passover, or wear leather. They were required to show humility by eating their food without salt, while seated on the ground.

Shabbatai Zevi had only made things worse. The Jews of Yemen needed a new Messiah and, as so often has been the case, a Messiah promptly arose to answer this need. The Yemenite Jews recognized Suleiman Jamal (d.1666) as the Messiah who would accomplish what Shabbatai had promised: to overcome the Muslims and lead the Return to Jerusalem.

During Passover of 1666, the Jews gathered in the synagogue

of San'a for a very special ceremony. They anointed Suleiman with perfume, dressed him in a regal silk gown, and prepared to march to their joint destiny. Suleiman Jamal was to lead them in procession to the governor's palace where he would seize the crown, just as the world had expected Shabbatai to seize the crown from the Sultan.

Unfortunately, the passion and unity evidenced in the synagogue ceremony began to dissipate as soon as the procession started to make its way through the city. At each crossroad along the way, more followers thought better of the adventure and dropped out. What began with much of the Jewish community of San'a ended with only Suleiman Jamal and two followers at the palace gates. Then these last two followers also fled, leaving Suleiman alone to face the governor.

The Messiah was not afraid. He confronted the governor alone and declared that the time had come for the transfer of sovereignty from the Muslims to the Jews. The governor was not afraid either. He had Suleiman imprisoned and tortured in an attempt to force him to convert to Islam. When Suleiman refused, he was sentenced to death. The Jewish community did what they could to avert the execution. They offered a large bribe for Suleiman's release, a maneuver that was often effective in such circumstances. When this was refused, they declared that God would punish any man who dared to execute the holy Messiah.

This last stratagem almost worked. All of the city's regular executioners refused to act. At the last minute, a man (said to be a descendant of Mohammed) with his head covered in disguise stepped forward and executed Suleiman Jamal. The Arabs dragged Suleiman's body through the streets, and his impaled head was displayed in public for three days until the Jews finally received permission to bury the body. Similar to the aftermath of Shlomo Molkho's death, the death of Suleiman Jamal was regarded by Yemenite Jews as holy martyrdom, and remembered as part of their local folklore. But Yemen's next major Messiah story eclipsed even the heroic story of the Messiah Suleiman Jamal.

It is understandable why many Jewish Messiahs suffered death by decapitation. It could be a humiliating form of death, as was intended in the execution of Suleiman Jamal. It provided a reliable means of identification of the victim and evidence that the execution had been carried out, and this evidence was in a form conveniently transportable to the ruler who had ordered the execution. Perhaps most importantly, in the era before modern medicine, decapitation conclusively established the fact of death. One Jewish Messiah managed to overcome this last presumption when he returned to his wife and followers after being beheaded. It could only have happened in Yemen.

Shukr ben Salim Kuhayl (c. 1821–1865), born Yehuda bar Shalom, was active as a Messiah in San'a, Yemen, from 1861 until his beheading in 1865. Present-day historians generally refer to him as "Shukr Kuhayl I" to distinguish him from the Messiah who returned after the beheading. Shukr Kuhayl I followed the familiar pattern of the Messiah-prophet. He began as a poor, modest scholar, travelling and preaching repentance. Then he claimed that Elijah had appeared to him and ordered him to divorce his wife so that he could devote himself to proclaiming to the Jews of Yemen that the Redemption was approaching. As many who proclaim such a message are, he was regarded by some Jews as mentally ill.

He soon expanded beyond his role as messenger and began to make claims to be the Messiah who was to initiate the Redemption. He displayed the words "Messiah of the line of David" written on his hand. He corrected the Bible's reference to the Messiah "Koresh," asserting that it was a scribal transposition and should be read to refer to the Messiah "Shukr."[36] He declared that he knew everything in the world, from the meaning of all the holy books to the secrets of everyone's heart. He claimed miraculous powers, including invulnerability to Muslim weapons. In the fashion of some holy men, he sat in isolation on a high tower in the desert. He won a very wide following because of his claims and especially because of his determined asceticism. Despite his popularity, he refused to accept money or even food and clothing from his followers, choosing instead an itinerant life of harsh austerity.

As he had written on his hand, he apparently believed that he was the Messiah of the House of David. To fulfil the conditions for his role, he predicted to the rabbis that the Messiah of the House of Joseph would appear and overthrow the Arab ruler within ninety days. Undiscouraged when his prediction failed, he continued to wander and preach repentance.

Finally, he had another vision, this time directing him to go up a mountain called al-Tiyal where he would disappear for a year before his return to the people. His excited followers discussed his ascension so much that word reached the King of San'a, who then sent his troops in pursuit. The troops returned in two days bearing the head of Shukr Kuhayl I. To put an end to the movement, the King had the head impaled and displayed for three days in the Jewish quarter of San'a.

As we have seen, putting an end to some Messiah movements may require more than merely the apparent evidence of the Messiah's death. The Jews' reaction to the display of Shukr Kuhayl I's head was not all that the King hoped for. Following the typical scenario, many followers simply didn't believe that Shukr was really dead. Some believed that he was fulfilling the role of the Messiah of the House of Joseph, who was supposed to fall in military conflict, but would be resurrected at the time of the Redemption. Others still trusted Shukr's promise that he would return from the mountain. As more than two years passed, many in the movement lost hope, but there remained a faithful core of followers who still believed and still waited. They were not entirely disappointed. The decapitated Shukr Kuhayl returned.

At least, a man claiming to be Shukr Kuhayl appeared in 1867. Although he is now called Shukr Kuhayl II by understandably skeptical historians, he was very popularly received at the time. He said he was Shukr. He went out to the desert and sat on Shukr's tower. The most dramatic confirmation of his claimed identity came when he declared that his earlier divorce had been conditional only, and he proceeded to resume living with the wife of Shukr Kuhayl I. Her recognition of the newly appeared Shukr as her husband became evident when she became pregnant.

Although this highly visible evidence of his wife's acceptance might ordinarily have been conclusive, many former critics and even followers of Shukr Kuhayl I still doubted. They seem to have had good reason to doubt. It is understandable that the experience of being beheaded is likely to change any man somewhat, but Shukr seemed to have changed a great deal.

For one thing, regardless of his wife's apparent satisfaction, his former followers noticed that he didn't look the same. He responded that he would soon transform himself into his familiar likeness, and perform other miracles. The people simply had to be patient until the time was ripe for him to start displaying his miraculous powers. That time of miracles never seemed to come. Shukr's explanation was that although he, of course, possessed the powers of miracle, Elijah had charged him not to exercise those powers until the people had sufficiently purified themselves through repentance and reformation. In short, Shukr was ready for miracles but the people weren't.

Shukr Kuhayl II had ready explanations for other challenges, also. Why had he not returned in one year, as he promised? He responded that he had indeed returned after one year, but had been wandering unrecognized among the people for the additional year and a half in order to gauge their readiness for the Reformation. Why had the scholarly Shukr ceased teaching and preaching

Torah? Again, his answer was that Elijah had forbidden him to teach Torah until the people made themselves ready and worthy to hear it. (In fact, Shukr Kuhayl II probably lacked Torah learning.)

Eventually it became time for this Messiah to begin the Reformation. At Passover, 1868, the word went out that Shukr was about to lead the Jews of San'a, together with the armies of some of the Lost Tribes, to conquer the Muslims. The local Jews were excited. The local Muslims were worried. The governor even directed the elders of the Jewish community to pray at the gravesites of prominent dead Jewish leaders to find out if Shukr was the true Messiah. It is not clear what answer they got, but in any event, the revolt never happened, and the San'a Jewish community escaped punishment for the disruption only at the price of the usual large bribe to the Muslim authorities. Shukr Kuhayl II then found it convenient to move his operations from San'a to al-Tawila.

It was at al-Tawila that a new issue regarding the true identity of Shukr Kuhayl II arose. Besides his changed appearance, it now appeared that in the course of his resurrection Shukr had also suffered significant changes in his character. A major factor in the popularity of Shukr Kuhayl I had been his dedicated asceticism, marked by his refusal to accepts gifts of funds, food, or clothing from his followers. It now seemed that Shukr's new head held different ideas. He not only accepted gifts, he demanded them.

He did not demand funds just from his local followers. Shukr Kuhayl II sent emissaries to the major Jewish communities in Palestine, India and Egypt demanding tithes (ma'aser). Shukr II claimed that these moneys were not for him, but to provide the Jewish community with an opportunity to practice righteousness, and thereby hasten the Redemption. In fact, he used the funds to support his grand court in al-Tawila where he fed hundreds of followers and visitors daily. He also redistributed some of the funds for relief of poor Jews and Muslims, and to pay the inevitable bribes to the Arab authorities. His letters demanding funds from the Jewish communities were signed and sealed with elaborate messianic flourishes—he described himself as "the holy one of heaven" or "His Excellency Master Shukr Kuhayl, may his kingdom endure forever."

Despite how transparently fraudulent he may seem to us, Shukr Kuhayl II was accepted by many (including some local Muslims) as the Messiah Shukr Kuhayl I, returned to begin the Reformation. Miracle stories circulated about his special relationship with Elijah, the messenger of the Messiah: Elijah had resurrected him after the decapitation. Elijah had forbidden him to perform miracles or teach Torah until the people proved themselves ready. Elijah had circumcised his newborn son. Elijah (rather than Shukr's bribe money) continued to work miracles to protect Shukr from assassination plots and military actions by the Arabs.

The greatest miracle, of course, was the initial one—Shukr's resurrection after being beheaded. He even bore the scar on his neck. (The chief rabbi of Yemen, Rabbi Amram Qorah, ultimately exposed how simply it was done: Shukr would stain his head and torso while a wool cord was tied around his neck, producing the white "scar" visible to the crowds.)

The inevitable downfall of Shukr Kuhayl II came from the powerful opposition of one man, the journalist Jacob Saphir, who wrote a series of critical, skeptical attacks against Shukr Kuhayl II in *Ha-Levanon,* the first Hebrew language newspaper in Palestine. Saphir even published his major attack under the title *Second Letter to Yemen* (1873), recalling Maimonides' criticism of the Yemenite Jewish community seven hundred years earlier. By winning the support of the Palestinian rabbis, Saphir's writings eventually destroyed Shukr's base of financial support in the Middle East. Without the tithe money, Shukr Kuhayl II lost his power to bribe the Arab officials, maintain his court, and dispense charity. He resorted to borrowing funds from Arab lenders to try to sustain his movement, but when he couldn't repay, he was imprisoned. He later died in his home in San'a, a Messiah without money, without power, and without followers.

Although even coming back after being beheaded was not enough of a miracle to maintain Shukr Kuhayl's movement to the end of his second life, his popularity was not totally lost. It seems that the Yemenite Jews have a certain fondness for their Messiahs regardless of the outcomes. The modern historian's careful distinction between Shukr Kuhayl I and Shukr Kuhayl II is not recognized in Yemenite folklore. The combined Messiah story of the resurrected Shukr Kuhayl can still be heard today in the traditional songs and folktales of Yemenite Jews living in modern Israel.

Shukr Kuhayl II's downfall and death did not end the Yemenites' adventures with Messiahs. A little later, yet another Messiah appeared in San'a. Around 1895 Yusuf Abdallah (Yosef Eved-El) began to preach the coming of the Messiah. Yusuf Abdallah declared that he had been sent to prepare the people for the Redemption and to work miracles. His principal miracle now appears to have been how much money he was able to get from the people as a means of preparing them for the Messiah.

Perhaps borrowing a technique from Shukr Kuhayl II, Yusuf Abdallah demanded gifts from his followers as the means of their purification in readiness for the Redemption. From the men, he got money, silver, and livestock, while the Jewish women gave him their fine clothing, jewelry and gold. What he couldn't obtain by donation from his followers, he borrowed from them, but— being otherwise unemployed—the Messiah could repay the old loans only by borrowing new funds.

Yusuf Abdallah was not a complicated Messiah. He spent all this money, as soon as it came in, on food, drink, and (reportedly) women, for himself and his followers. The theology of his movement was likewise uncomplicated. Although he took some steps to revise prayers and holiday celebrations, he did not teach or preach. Indeed, his most prominent reputation for public speaking came from his practice of making braying noises to his followers while they were drinking at night, which they would then similarly answer.

The Yemenite rabbis were not fooled by the bald fraud being practiced by Yusuf Abdallah, but to deal with it they had to turn to the civil government. Acting on the rabbis' complaints, the Ottoman government finally expelled Yusuf Abdallah, ending the last major Jewish Messiah movement of the nineteenth century.

Chapter 24

TODAY'S MESSIAH

It is clear that many of those followers who during his lifetime believed that Rabbi Schneerson was the Messiah still hold that belief.

W E ARE now beginning a new millennium in an era of advanced scientific knowledge. Modern education and communications transmit this knowledge to the general public. Nevertheless, the new scientific era has not seen the end of the Jewish Messiah stories. Even though the year 2000 CE had no millennial significance for Jews (for whom it simply constituted part of years 5760 and 5761), the increased exuberance of Christian millenarians at the end of the twentieth century has helped to heat up Jewish messianic hopes also.

Most significant for messianic hopes of both Christians and Jews is the fact that, in the second half of the twentieth century, Jews from all over the world have returned to the Promised Land to establish the Jewish State of Israel. This has not been accomplished precisely in accordance with the predictions of the Jewish messianic myth. No Messiah has carried the Jews to Israel or led them in the military battles necessary to win the land. Still, many Christians and Jews believe that the establishment of the State of Israel satisfies one of the critical preconditions for the messianic era.

In modern Israel, this—like almost everything else—has become a political issue. After two thousand years, some Jews are still trying to hasten the Redemption by forcing fulfillment of the prerequisites. If the Bible says that Jews are supposed to have sovereignty over the Promised Land before the Messiah comes, then to some believers it is clear that this must refer to the ancient biblical boundaries. They transform this conclusion into a drive to expand modern Israel to acquire additional territory beyond the allocation from the United Nations and beyond the accretion from several wars. Israel even has a formal political party, Gush Emunim (Block of the Faithful), dedicated to having Israel acquire and hold all the land to the biblical borders.

Twentieth century Judaism also had (and for some, twenty-first century Judaism still has) a specific Messiah—the Lubavitcher rebbe Menachem Mendel Schneerson (1902–1994), the seventh rebbe of the Lubavitch sect of Hasidism (popularly known as Chabad). Rabbi Schneerson was born in Nikolayev, Russia, and educated at the Sorbonne. He married the daughter of Yosepf Yitzhak Schneersohn, the head of the Lubavitch sect, and succeeded his father-in-law in 1951 as leader of Lubavitch-Chabad.

Under Rabbi Schneerson's leadership, Chabad focused on the importance of each Jew's efforts to observe ritual obligations and commandments as a means of hastening the coming of the Messiah. Chabad's slogan is "Moshiach (Messiah) Now!" The movement established and maintains community social welfare services and educational and religious programs in over one hundred countries throughout the world. Its high profile and active recruitment efforts have attracted many new followers among worldwide Jewry.

Although there is some controversy over the extent to which

Rabbi Schneerson expressly asserted that he was the Messiah, it is clear that he spoke and acted in a manner that led a significant faction of his followers to believe it. He gave his followers directions on a variety of personal issues, including important decisions regarding their health care, investments, and family and personal relationships. (His advice was often based upon the need for precise fulfillment of some ritual requirement, such as correcting the lettering of the miniature scroll inside a mezuzah— the small container holding a scroll with three biblical passages, placed on the doorways of Jewish homes). He was the center of many miracle tales.

Shneur Zalman (1745–1813), the founder of Lubavitch, predicted that the messianic era would be the Sabbath of the world, meaning that it would begin in the seventh millennium. Because the year 6001 in the Hebrew calendar (which begins the seventh millennium) will fall in the year 2241, Rabbi Schneerson calculated that we should soon begin to feel the early signs of the coming messianic era. He even saw the Persian Gulf War (1990–1991) as the start of the worldwide civil unrest that is to be the precursor to the Messiah's appearance. In confirmation of his confidence in the imminence of the Messiah, Rabbi Schneerson stated that it was not a problem that he left no descendents and would therefore be the last Lubavitch rebbe. None would be needed after him.

Based upon all of this, a faction of the Chabad movement was certain that the Messiah who was about to reveal himself to the world was Schneerson himself. The consequences of Rabbi Schneerson's death in 1994 for the Chabad movement, and especially for the messianic faction of followers who believe that he is the Messiah, is still working itself out. It is clear that many of those followers who during his lifetime believed that Rabbi Schneerson was the Messiah still hold that belief. Some accept the fact of his death on the grounds that he was the Messiah of his generation, but that he was not permitted to bring about the messianic era because the people were not yet sufficiently worthy through universal and full observance of mitzvot.

Other messianic followers deny that Rabbi Schneerson has died, or insist that he will return as soon as the people fulfil the conditions for the messianic age to begin. They make pilgrimage to his grave, venerate his picture, and celebrate him in their prayers. They still seek and follow his advice for their current life decisions by randomly selecting a letter from the records of his lifetime correspondence—whatever their problem, they insert a marker into his collected correspondence and are guided by his earlier answer that they find there.

It has been reported that the Chabad home office in Crown Heights, New York, has become physically divided. Those who believe that Schneerson is the Messiah stay downstairs, meeting and praying, while those who do not so believe stay upstairs, managing the institutional operations. Interaction between the two factions is said to be dwindling.

Thus, at the onset of the twenty-first century, Jewish messianic beliefs continue with traditional vigor, even though the most recent Messiah, Menachem Mendel Schneerson, operated and achieved in ways far different from his predecessor Messiahs. He was educated in a fine secular university. He built up an organization that uses the latest in modern technology, communications, and business techniques in order to sustain and grow its movement. His advice was sought and relied upon in complex modern medical, financial, and personal matters. Far from being a Messiah of desperate times for the Jews, he gained a dedicated following in America during a period of unprecedented general economic prosperity, when Jews' ability to participate in business and government seemed almost unlimited.

The twentieth century also uniquely satisfied the principal conditions to the messianic era. If the Messiah is to be preceded by birth pangs, the Holocaust unquestionably qualifies. Rabbi Schneerson's lifetime also witnessed the return of the Jews to sovereignty in Israel.

The past two thousand years of Jewish Messiahs have produced a few martyrs and heroes but, it sadly appears, a far greater share of confidence men, thieves, madmen, and innocents. Past messianic movements have generally brought disillusionment and disaster to the Jewish communities involved. We await the judgment of the twenty-first century on this latest Jewish Messiah.

CONCLUSION

HOW SHOULD we deal with these two thousand years of Jewish Messiah stories? Basically, I believe that we should simply accept and enjoy them. These stories *are*. They may interweave fantasy with fact, but the problematic reality of some of the stories' content is a very different issue from the unquestioned reality of the stories' existence and impact.

The stories themselves—even the wildest of them—are a form of historical truth, in the sense that they were believed by a significant segment of the Jewish and non-Jewish worlds at the time. The stories affected people and influenced the course of history. This aspect of the stories' importance transcends the question of which story elements are true and which are fable.

The stories also provide fresh insight into the interconnectedness of earlier Jewish and non-Jewish societies. The Jewish Messiah stories reveal repeated instances when the highest levels of the Catholic, Protestant, Muslim, and secular worlds were caught up in Jewish messianic excitement, even to the point of active participation by kings, popes, and emperors. This often occurred in periods when the Jewish community was otherwise without power or influence in the general society.

The effects of the stories also demonstrate the speed with which ideas could travel before modern communication. Even without the telegraph, telephone, radio, steamships, automobiles, or airplanes, it was possible for news of seventeenth century Messiah events to reach around the globe in a matter of weeks, depending solely upon commercial sailing ships and overland travelers. Once foreign news arrived in the various Jewish communities, communal readings in the synagogue, dissemination through printed materials, and transmission through established links of private correspondence were able to spread the news locally almost immediately.

In addition, after appreciating both the effects of the Jewish Messiah stories on general history and what those stories can tell us about general history, I believe we can learn much from considering why it was that century after century of Jews have continued to believe their new Messiah stories. Analysis of the Messiahs' histories shows two recurrent factors that seem to have set the groundwork for the appearance of most of the Jewish Messiahs: messianic calculations and hard times. These two factors operated similarly, by creating a heightened sense of expectation.

Messianic calculations expressly raise the level of awareness and anticipation. From the eighty-fifth Jubilee prediction preceding Moses of Crete in 440, to the seventh millennium prediction preceding Menachem Mendel Schneerson in 1994, the people have been primed to expect their Messiahs according to schedule.

The almost universal adoption of the "birth pangs" theory likewise functioned through expectation. For a people repeatedly subjected to periods of harsh oppression and miserable circumstances, a doctrine that such suffering is to be followed (if not rewarded) by messianic salvation would regularly raise fervent messianic expectation.

At various times, the combined effects of calculation and birth pangs were intensified by other factors, including the popularity of philosophical and theological theories (such as Lurianic Kabbalism) emphasizing the coming of the Messiah. At other times, contemporary Catholic, Protestant, or Muslim messianic concerns have reinforced Jewish expectations. Finally, the ground for a new Jewish Messiah was often prepared by the popularity of a preceding messianic movement, especially when it had appeared in the same geographic area.

Such an analysis only identifies the several elements contributing to the timing and intensity of the people's response to their Messiahs. The central question remains: Why did the Jews believe in any Messiah at any time? On the surface, at least, such belief appears contrary to common sense and certainly contrary to the people's repeated experience of previous disappointments. Some of the Jewish Messiah stories are ludicrous while others are tragic. Why did such repeated debacles fail to discourage further messianic movements?

I believe that the Jewish belief in Messiah has been more than a "desperation theology"—more than a knee-jerk reaction to the pain of adversity. The people's belief in a Messiah was a genuine expression of faith, an undertaking of optimism. For another people, perhaps, hard times could as easily have led to pessimism, depression, and paralysis—even the end of the people. The Jewish response of messianic hope has provided a mechanism for coping, a tool for survival.

Viewed in this light, the Jews' repeated engagements with their two thousand years of Messiahs have played a part in the people's remarkable ability to overcome the severest challenges. At the outset of this book, I stated that the Jewish Messiah stories are relatively unknown today because of communal shame. When the act of stubbornly clinging to a belief system helps save a people, it should not be shameful. Stubborn optimism is still optimism.

If the lessons of history foreshadow the future, we can expect that our twenty-first century will bring new Jewish Messiahs, each of whom will provide his or her individual mix of holiness and demagoguery, inspiration and disappointment, to a Jewish community that eternally prays for the messianic blessings of peace for the world. Someday, those new Jewish Messiah stories will also be told.

ENDNOTES

INTRODUCTION

[1] The term "Talmud" generally refers to a combination of two bodies of rabbinic commentaries. The Mishnah, which was consolidated by the early third century, records generations of rabbinic expression of the "Oral Law," the revelations of law received by Moses in addition to the written Torah. The Gemara contains commentaries on the Mishnah by later generations of scholars. It was completed in about the fifth or sixth century.

There are actually two versions of the Talmud. The earlier one, compiled in Palestine, is known as the Jerusalem (or Land of Israel) Talmud, while the later, larger, and more organized Babylonian Talmud is more accessible for contemporary readers. (In this book, unless the Jerusalem Talmud is expressly indicated, references to the Talmud are to the Babylonian Talmud.)

Talmud study is often supplemented by examination of later commentaries, including extensive interpretation by the great Rashi (Rabbi Shlomo Itzhaki, 1040–1105), supplementary analysis by Rashi's disciples and later generations (Tosafot), and selected commentaries by other medieval and later sages.

[2] The specter of the Jews suffering the birth pangs preceding the Messiah was so awesome that several rabbis of the Talmud (Rabbis Ulla, Rabbah, and Johanan) welcomed the coming of the Messiah, but prayed that they personally would not be alive to witness the suffering: "Let him come, but let me not see him."

[3] Early reference to the two-Messiah concept has been found in the Qumran "Dead Sea" Scrolls. The Messiah of the House of Joseph is sometimes specifically identified as descending

from Joseph's son, Ephraim. In biblical and rabbinic terminology, "Ephraim" often refers collectively to the Ten Tribes of the northern Kingdom of Israel. Thus, the doctrine that there will be two Messiahs, one descended from Ephraim and one from David (who was a member of the tribe of Judah, which became the southern Kingdom of Judah), may express that the Redemption will include reunification of the two kingdoms of Israel and Judah.

4 The later prophetic writings added other important features to the Jewish messianic idea, such as the concepts that Elijah will be the advance messenger of the messianic era and that the End of Days will witness the resurrection of the dead.

5 For the argument against using the terms "false Messiah" or "pseudo-Messiah," see Saperstein, ed., *Essential Papers,* pp. 4-5.

CHAPTER 1

6 For an expanded discussion of who could be regarded as the First Messiah, see Appendix A: Note on Selecting the First Messiah.

7 The Jews' initial excitement and ultimate disappointment over Hadrian's promise to rebuild the Temple may have been specially driven by a particular aspect of messianic belief—Jewish legend states that the Messiah will announce the Redemption from the roof of the Temple.

8 At a time when most of the leading rabbis had begun their studies in childhood as prodigies or descendants of generations of scholars, Rabbi Akiba was an uneducated shepherd who only late in life began decades of study to earn his respected position.

9 In contemporary idiom, the phrase "grass will sooner grow on your chin" would be like telling someone "you'll be pushing up daisies" (you'll be dead) long before the Messiah will come.

10 The Talmud not only fixes the 9th day of the month of Av as

the day for the tragedies of the fall of the First and Second Temples and the capture of Betar, as well as many other national disasters in Jewish history, it also explains the reason why God chose that date. When ten of the twelve spies sent by Moses to reconnoiter the land of Canaan returned with a falsely pessimistic report, the Israelites were quick to despair, ignoring the positive reports of Caleb and Joshua and refusing to trust in God. The Bible describes how the people reacted to the spies' negative report: "...the people wept that night." (Num. 14:1.) The rabbis of the Talmud concluded "that night" was the 9th of Av, and imagine God responding to the people, "You have wept without cause; therefore I will set the day aside for weeping throughout the generations to come."

CHAPTER 3

11 Some rabbinic laws expressed in the Talmud elaborate, extend, and add to the basic laws of the Bible. This was often seen as necessary in order to "place a fence around the Torah"—i.e., to avoid even inadvertent violation of basic laws by imposing more stringent rabbinic standards. In the messianic era, people would be living in a state of universal goodness, so there would be no need for rabbinic rules to protect the biblical laws.

CHAPTER 5

12 Although calculation of the time for the coming of the Messiah was a major rabbinic enterprise, Maimonides had strong Talmudic support for condemning the practice: "Blasted be the bones of those who calculate the End."

CHAPTER 6

13 Maimonides' identification of the locale of the Lyons

Messiah has led to an eight hundred-year dispute as to what city he was describing. Maimonides said that the incident occurred in the city of Linon in the country of Ifranja (the "land of the Franks"). Until recently, most historians read that to mean the city of Lyons, in France. Now some have pointed out that in Maimonides' time Arab geographers also called Spain the land of the Franks. They also note that, since Maimonides' family came from Cordoba, he may be more likely to have heard the history of this incident if it had happened in Spain. On this basis, many current scholars have concluded that the "Lyons Messiah" actually appeared in Leon, Spain, rather than Lyons, France.

CHAPTER 7

[14] We know the story of the disputation in Khazaria primarily through the tenth century report of King Joseph of Khazaria replying to a letter from Hisdai ibn Shaprut, a Spanish Jew. Yehudah Halevi, a Jewish philosopher and poet of the eleventh and twelfth centuries, also dramatized the debate in his work, *Kuzari*. Although the national conversion to Judaism is amply historically documented, the story of the disputation may be only a fanciful elaboration on the fact that Judaism was a politically savvy choice for a nation seeking neutral status between its two powerful neighbors, the Byzantine Christian Empire and Muslim Baghdad (see Blady, *Jewish Communities*, p. 116).

CHAPTER 8

[15] Some modern scholars have challenged the accuracy of several points of the traditional Abulafia story. For example, some historians conclude that Abraham Abulafia may have received only a single revelation, and that he eventually went to the pope simply to plead for the Jews or to engage in a

philosophical debate over the respective merits of Christianity and Judaism. Also, he may have failed actually to meet with Pope Nicholas before the pope suddenly died (see Idel, *Messianic Mystics*, pp. 97-99). Nevertheless, the traditional story recounted in this chapter was the one accepted at the time by Abulafia's followers and much of the rest of the Jewish world. Even Abulafia himself was sufficiently impressed by his own legend that he later claimed that he had intentionally caused the pope's death by uttering the name of God.

16 Yitzhak Baer, in his *History of the Jews*, not only relates the story told in this chapter of Nissim ben Abraham, the Prophet of Avila, but also tells an essentially identical story about a prophet called Samuel of Ayllon (Spain), also in 1295. The origin for the Avila story is Rabbi Adret, who read and rejected the prophet's writings. The source of the double stories of Avila and Ayllon is Abner, Bishop of Burgos, Spain, who was far from being an unbiased observer of Jewish events.

Bishop Abner began his ecclesiastic career as Solomon Ha-Levi, the chief Rabbi of Burgos. He converted to Catholicism in 1390 (even before the violence of the 1391 pogroms). After his Church studies in France, he returned and was made the Bishop of Burgos. It is therefore not surprising that the bishop's Avila and Ayllon stories feature strong anti-Semitic elements (when the Messiah fails to materialize, crosses miraculously appear on the white garments of the Jews). Because of the questionable source of the double stories, and in any event in light of the suspiciously close similarities between the two, the version ascribed to Samuel of Ayllon is not repeated in this chapter.

CHAPTER 9

17 The popular term Marrano was initially a pejorative name (perhaps derived from an early word meaning swine) for Jewish families who had converted to Christianity in Portugal at the time of the Inquisition. The neutral term Converso, now used primarily for Spanish converts, could also be used to describe Iberian converts generally. The formal Christian term for these families was "New Christians."

A substantial number of Converso and Marrano families retained some Jewish observances for many generations. Some families resumed Judaism upon emigrating to Holland, Turkey, Palestine, and elsewhere. Other converts or their descendents achieved prominence in the Church and government, including Rabbi Solomon Ha-Levi, who became the Catholic Bishop of Burgos, and Joshua Ha-Lorki, who became Heronimo de Santa Fe, leader of the anti-Jewish attack in the Disputation of Tortosa (1413–1414). It is generally believed that famous descendents of Conversos included King Philip I of Castile (1478–1506), son-in-law of Ferdinand and Isabella; the Grand Inquisitor Thomas de Torquemada (1420–1498); his successor Diego Deza (served 1499–1507); and Santa Theresa of Avila (1515–1582), founder of the Reformed Order of Carmelites.

CHAPTER 13

[18] Ethiopia, in northern Africa, is the land of ancient Abyssinia. For an expanded discussion of the Beta Israel and some of the other current candidates for recognition as members of the Ten Tribes, see Appendix B: Note on the Beta Israel and the Ten Tribes.

[19] David Reuveni's initial appearance in Rome on a splendid white horse may have been designed to echo the Christian Bible prophecy of St. John the Divine that the first of the millennial seven seals will mark the crowned warrior on a white horse. A fifteenth century painting of Jesus on a white horse was one of the illustrations in Newsweek magazine's November 1, 1999 cover story on millennial prophecy.

CHAPTER 14

20 For the view that Molkho—even without pre-conversion Jewish studies—could have learned sufficient Kabbalah during his brief time in the Ottoman Empire to support his homiletic preaching, see Idel, *Messianic Mystics*, p. 145.

21 There are two conflicting versions of the Messiah's appearance—he will appear either magnificently (like David Reuveni) on a great white horse, or in humility (like Shlomo Molkho) riding on a lowly donkey. An example of the latter version can be seen in one of the illustrations for the Encyclopedia Judaica CD-ROM article on "Messiah." The illustration displays a replica of an illuminated manuscript with the caption: "The messiah arriving on a white donkey at the gates of Jerusalem preceded by Elijah blowing a shofar to announce his arrival."

22 Contrary to current popular perception, the Inquisition was a Catholic institution that did not have jurisdiction to punish non-Catholics including Jews (except for certain universal crimes against the Catholic religion, such as blasphemy). Inquisition jurisdiction only attached once a Jew purported to convert to Catholicism. The convert and all his descendents were then subject to full church law, including the capital ban against "Judaising" (lapsing into Jewish observances).

23 For an expanded discussion of the limitations on Pope Clement's power at this time, see Appendix C: Note on the Power Conflicts among Pope Clement VII, Emperor Charles V, and King Henry VIII.

24 "Except for Jesus, he [Shlomo Molkho] was the most influential Jewish Messiah to date." Idel, *Messianic Mystics*, p. 151.

CHAPTER 15

25 Although the major portions of the Zohar assert that they are statements by Simeon bar Yohai and his contemporaries from the second century, the work is generally believed to have been written by various Spanish and Portuguese Jewish scholars. It was then assembled and published in Spain by Moses de Leon at the end of the thirteenth century.

CHAPTER 16

26 In the ninth century a man named Eldad ha-Dani appeared, claiming to be a member of the tribe of Dan, which he said had joined with three other of the Ten Tribes near Ethiopia. In the twelfth century Benjamin of Tudela, the same author who secured the fame of the Messiah David Alroy, also wrote detailed descriptions of seven of the Lost Tribes, based on stories he had heard from Persian Jews. According to Benjamin's report, the four tribes of Dan, Asher, Zebulun, and Naphtali lived in Nishapur (a town in northern Persia), while the tribes of Reuben and Gad and the half-tribe of Manasseh lived in Khaybar, Arabia. In the sixteenth century, the Messiah David Reuveni may have simply adopted the report of Benjamin of Tudela when Reuveni claimed that he was the general of the armies of Reuben, Gad, and Manasseh, living near Khaybar.

27 Although the Sambatyon River was supposed to be seventeen miles wide, some travelers claimed that they had seen or even communicated with the Tribes by managing to find one place where it narrowed to shouting distance.

According to the rabbis, the Ten Tribes had been exiled beyond the Sambatyon River in order to save them until the time of Redemption. Rabbi Akiba cited the weekly schedule of the "Sabatyon" River as proof that Saturday was the true Sabbath.

For an interesting collection of writings about the Sambatyon, see Shtull-Trauring, *Letters*, with its accompanying CD-ROM about the Ten Tribes.

28 The historian Josephus (30–100 CE) records in passing that Titus saw the Sambatyon ("Sabbatical") River in Syria. Josephus's version is reversed from other accounts. He states that the river flows only on the Sabbath and is dry the other six days of the week (which misses the point of how it could serve as a barrier isolating the Ten Tribes). The other sources regarding the Sambatyon generally agree with Pliny's first century report that "In Iudea rivus sabbatis omnibus siccatur" ("In Judea is a stream that dries up every Sabbath").

29 Manasseh ben Israel's theory of how the Lost Tribes (and the rest of the native Americans) came to the Americas was brilliantly ahead of its time. Manasseh proposed that after the Exile in 722 BCE some of the Tribes had settled in Asia. They later fled to the New World, pursued by the Tartars, over a then-existing land bridge between Russia and Alaska. That land bridge subsequently flooded to form the waters visible in Manasseh's time, now called the Bering Straight.

It is generally accepted today that the Americas were indeed populated by peoples coming across that land bridge, although this is now ascribed to the ice age of the Pleistocene Epoch, which ended ten thousand years ago.

30 Cromwell was clearly influenced to readmit the Jews to England in order to satisfy the intense Puritan interest in fulfilling the messianic prophecy of the Hebrew Bible so that Jesus' Second Coming could occur. This might not have been his sole reason. The Protectorate might also have been interested in securing the financial abilities of the expelled Jewish money lenders to help replenish England's wealth, which had been exhausted by the Civil War (see Picard, *Restoration London*, p. 269).

CHAPTER 17

31 Shabbatai Zevi was the greatest of the Jewish Messiahs even though he did the greatest injury to the Jewish people. Huge contrasts separate him from all of the Jewish Messiahs who preceded him. The others generally had only a local following. Shabbatai inflamed as much as one-half of the Jews of the world. The other Messiahs founded movements that generally died with them, or at most left a core of believers over a few subsequent generations. A group of Shabbatai's followers went underground in the seventeenth century and their secret sect continued well into the twentieth century. The others left only fragments of legends, folk-tales, and historically unreliable reports telling about their lives. Modern scholars (in particular, Gershom Scholem) have exhaustively researched Shabbatai's history. The other Messiahs remain essentially unknown to the typical contemporary Jew, but at least the basic elements of Shabbatai's reign as Messiah and its shameful aftermath are widely known today.

[32] According to the American Psychiatric Association's *Manual of Mental Disorders* (p. 328), manic episodes of Bipolar Affective Disorder may display "inflated self-esteem or grandiosity." "Grandiose delusions are common (e.g., having a special relationship to God...)." "The individual may become theatrical, with dramatic mannerisms and singing." The mean age for onset of the first manic episode is in the early twenties (p. 331).

CHAPTER 20

[33] The Donmeh's eighteen commandments transformed the biblical prohibition against adultery into a concern for public reputation: "There shall be among them no adulterers. Although this is [only] a commandment of the Created World, because of the thieves it is necessary to be scrupulous [in observance]." Scholem, "The Sprouting of the Horn," p. 384.

CHAPTER 21

34 History has judged Jacob Frank in the harshest of terms: "...[T]here can be no doubt that Jacob Frank ... was an out-and-out fake." Dimont, Jews, *God and History*, p. 277.

"Jacob Frank and his followers . . . were tainted with grossness and moral corruption...." Silver, *A History of Messianic Speculation*, 1959 Preface, p. xv.

"Jacob Frank (1726–91) will always be remembered as one of the most frightening phenomena in the whole of Jewish history; a religious leader who, whether for purely self-interested motives or otherwise, was in all his actions a truly corrupt and degenerate individual." Scholem, "Redemption through Sin" in *The Messianic Idea in Judaism*, p. 126.

CHAPTER 22

35 The impact of Hasidism on Jewish messianism bears a parallel to the earlier impact of Lurianic Kabbalism. Both movements expressed a concern for redemption through individual activity rather than through the actions of the Messiah. Lurianic Kabbalism focused on tikun (repair), individual efforts to perform mitzvot (biblical commandments). Hasidism emphasized individual redemption through a joyous personal relationship with God.

CHAPTER 23

36 "Koresh" is referred to in the verse: "Thus said God to his anointed one, to Koresh...." (Isa. 45:1.) Koresh is the biblical name for Cyrus the Great, King of Persia (r. 559–529 BCE), who is referred to in the Bible as anointed by God (a Messiah) because he ended the Babylonian exile and permitted the Jews to rebuild the Second Temple in Jerusalem.

America is still dealing with the aftermath of a modern-day Messiah Koresh. David Koresh (who selected his double-messianic name when he changed his name from Vernon Howell) and seventy-nine of his Branch Davidian followers died in the fire at their Waco, Texas compound while resisting the government on April 19, 1993. Two years later America suffered the bombing of the Oklahoma City federal government office building on the anniversary of Waco. Six years after Waco, the FBI admitted lying to Congress and the public about the use of incendiary devices in the 1993 attack, triggering a new independent investigation into the Clinton/Reno Justice Department's handling of the matter. It remains to be seen whether the recent conclusion of that investigation can put a final end to the theories and accusations of a skeptical anti-government movement still critical of the government's actions at Waco.

APPENDIX

APPENDIX A: Note on Selecting the First Messiah

People like neatness; history doesn't. Even the question of who was the first Jewish Messiah after Jesus cannot be answered without some controversy. First, we can note that there were several possible Jewish Messiahs who appeared even before Jesus.

One expert on the Dead Sea Scrolls has recently proposed that a prophet, whom he calls "Judah," referred to in the Scrolls as the "Teacher of Righteousness," deserves to be called the first Jewish Messiah (see Wise, *The First Messiah*). Active in the first century BCE, the Teacher of Righteousness was apparently regarded as a Messiah by some Jews but as a heretic by others. If he was the first Jewish Messiah, his movement and its impact on Jews and the world have not previously been generally recognized.

Perhaps the earliest significant biblical references to a particular Messiah are in the writings of the prophet Zechariah. Zechariah's description of the Messiah is generally understood to refer to Zerubbabel (the prophet Haggai's messianic reference to Zerubbabel is explicit). Zerubbabel, a descendant of King David, was a Babylonian exile who returned to become the governor of Jerusalem in about 519 BCE. Since little more is known about him or his impact, he also makes a poor candidate for the title of First Messiah.

In contrast, another possibility for first Jewish Messiah is a universally known figure—Judah Maccabee, the hero of the Chanukah story of 164 BCE. Maccabee's story displays many of the elements commonly expected from a Messiah: He was a bold and charismatic military chief who led the successful Jewish rebellion against the Syrian Selucids. He became king of the Jews, and established the one hundred-year Hasmonean dynasty. Finally, he is associated with an important miracle (the familiar Chanukah story of the single day's consecrated oil that kept the menorah lamp burning for eight days). Despite these messianic features, the Maccabee story is not truly a Messiah story. Judah Maccabee was not descended from the Davidic line (or even from the Davidic priestly line of Zadok), and never claimed to be the Messiah.

Judah Maccabee does not appear to have developed followers who believed he was the Messiah. Indeed, in their commentary on the Chanukah festival, the rabbis of the Talmud seem to have gone out of their way to minimize his personal heroic qualities and instead emphasize God's miraculous intervention.

Similarly, Simon ben Gioras, John ben Levy, Eleazar ben Simon, and Menahem ben Judas led their respective "Zealot" factions in the first century Jewish revolt leading to the destruction of the Second Temple in 70 CE and the fall of Masada in 73 CE. Despite developing fanatically loyal followings and establishing competing claims for kingship over the Jews, none of these military leaders or their followers made significant messianic claims, produced miracles, or preached the utopian End of Days. Like Judah Maccabee, therefore, they fall outside of our working definition of a Jewish Messiah (but see Horsely, "Popular Messianic Movements," in Saperstein, ed., *Essential Papers*, pp. 98-103).

One possible first Jewish Messiah appearing after Jesus perhaps does deserve to be called a Messiah. The Jewish historian Josephus recounts the adventures of Theudas, who was active in the year 44 CE. During the time of Roman oppression under Procurator Cuspis Fadus, a man named Theudas undertook to save his followers in a highly dramatic fashion. If they would follow him to the banks of the Jordan, the prophet-magician promised to part the waters so the people could escape the Romans by walking across the dry riverbed. (As precedent for the power of a prophet to split the Jordan, he could point to the Bible stories of Joshua, Elijah and Elisha.)

Perhaps influenced by the successful escape of Moses' followers at the Red Sea, several hundred believers apparently followed Theudas to his proposed reversal of the Exodus—this time to flee from the Promised Land, rather than to it. The Roman cavalry proved more effective than the Egyptian charioteers, and they caught up with the procession before Theudas had a chance to do his magic. Many of the followers were captured or killed. In a conclusion that has echoed through many subsequent Messiah stories, Theudas was decapitated and his head was returned to Jerusalem. Little else is known about this incident. Josephus does not record whether Theudas claimed that he was the Messiah, or was so regarded by his band of believers.

The stories of Judah Maccabee and the Zealot leaders relate impressive military activity but do not show sufficient messianic claims or beliefs. The Teacher of Righteousness, Zerubbabel, and Theudas may qualify to be considered Messiahs, but none of them demonstrated the combination of messianic claims, popular support, and enduring legend to be singled out as the first Jewish Messiah. Based on this, the text names Simeon Bar Kokhba as the first Jewish Messiah since Jesus.

APPENDIX B: Note on the Beta Israel and the Ten Tribes

The Beta Israel ethnic group claim that they were descended from ten thousand Jews of King Solomon's court who returned to Ethiopia with Menelek, the son of Solomon and the Queen of Sheba. Although the Beta Israel apparently lacked access to the Talmud, they possessed a translation of the Hebrew Bible and some of the Apocrypha, and observed many Jewish rituals such as daily synagogue prayers, kashrut dietary laws, eighth day circumcision, the Jewish Sabbath and biblical holidays, ritual bathing, a week of wedding festivities, immediate burial of the dead, and seven days of mourning.

In 1984 and 1990, the State of Israel carried out "Operation Moses" and "Operation Solomon," airlifting most of the remaining 20,000 Beta Israel members from Ethiopia to their new home in Israel. There they joined a roughly equal number of recent Beta Israel immigrants. In Operation Moses and Operation Solomon, truth proved stranger than legend: after two millennia, a "lost" tribe of Jews indeed returned to the Promised Land on the wings of angels.

For a recent analysis of the Beta Israel history and claim to Jewish ethnicity, see Blady, *Jewish Communities*, Part 14, pp. 347-90.

The question of the identity of the Ten Tribes persists today. For example, unlike the legend that underlies the claims of the Beta Israel of Ethiopia, the latest techniques of modern science seem to support the claim of another tribe, the Lemba of southern Africa, that their ancestors came from Judea. The tribe observes a weekly Sabbath, does not eat pork, and practices circumcision. DNA testing shows that 53% of the priestly Bhuba clan of the Lemba carry the distinctive genetic markers for descendents of the Kohen priestly tribe of the Jews. This matches the expression of those genetic markers in the general population of Jewish Kohanim.

Similarly, various other tribes and groups around the world have been proposed as candidates for the Lost Tribes, including the Pathans in the Afghanistan/Pakistan/Kashmir region, the Samurai (Samarians?) of Japan, and the Chiang-Min of Szechwan, China. Extensive information related to the recent NOVA television program on the Lost Tribes is available on the internet at www.pbs.org.

The immigration policy of the State of Israel is currently being challenged by the Bnai Menashe, members of a Burmese–Indian tribe that have converted to orthodox Judaism and believe that they are descendents of one of the Lost Tribes. When discovered in the nineteenth century, the tribe already possessed songs and stories apparently retelling the biblical story of the Jews' Exodus from Egypt.

APPENDIX C: Note on the Power Conflicts among Pope Clement VII, Emperor Charles V, and King Henry VIII

It may seem odd today that Pope Clement VII could not control his own Catholic Inquisition in order to protect the Messiah Shlomo Molkho against Emperor Charles V, but this was not the most significant occasion when Charles's military power trumped Clement's papal authority. Just prior to Molkho's death, the emperor and the pope struggled over the demand of England's King Henry VIII for an annulment of marriage from his first wife, Catherine of Aragon, so that he could marry Anne Boleyn. (Catherine, "the Spanish Queen" of England, was the daughter of Ferdinand and Isabella, who had expelled the Jews from Spain in 1492.)

As a major prince of the Church, Henry had great influence over Pope Clement and might have obtained the annulment he sought except for one important detail: Emperor Charles was Catherine's nephew. Charles's army had already triumphed over Clement in the sack of Rome in 1527. Clement had to flee Rome for Orvietto. Fear of further imperial military attack influenced Clement to refuse to grant the annulment. Henry's response was to take England out of the Catholic Church and establish the Church of England. This permitted him to marry Anne Boleyn, and their daughter ultimately reigned as Queen Elizabeth I.

This great Christian church dispute also had a more direct Jewish connection—it was formally waged over competing Jewish theological doctrines. Before marrying Henry, Catherine had been widowed, childless, upon the death in 1502 of her first husband, Henry's brother Arthur. Henry justified his demand for an annulment of his marriage to Catherine on the grounds that the marriage was invalid under Lev. 18:16 ("Thou shalt not uncover the nakedness of thy brother's wife").

Henry's opponents supported the validity of the marriage by

citing the Jewish practice of levirate marriage (the obligation to marry a childless brother's widow in order to perpetuate his line and inheritance, Deut. 25:5-10). It could certainly be argued that Henry had energetically striven to fulfill any such obligation to Arthur. By the time of the annulment, Catherine had produced five stillbirths, one child who died in infancy, and Mary Tudor, who succeeded to the throne of England after the death of the young Edward VI.

DEFINITIONS

WHERE CONVENIENT, terms have been briefly defined in the text the first time they are used. The following are restatements or expansions of those definitions:

am haaretz   Lit., a man of the soil. Not an intellectual; a simple man.

Ashkenazi   Referring to the sub-group of Jews originally settling in Germany, and subsequently spreading to Poland, Russia and Western Europe. The rituals, language, laws, and customs of Ashkenazi Jews and their descendents often differ from those of the other major sub-group, Sephardi Jews (originally from Spain and Portugal, and who spread to the Middle East, Turkey, Italy, and North Africa after the Expulsion Orders of 1492 and 1497).

birth pangs   A central element of popular Jewish messianic belief holding that the messianic era will be preceded by a time of worldwide chaos and destruction and, in particular, terrible suffering for the Jews.

Black Madonna The revered painting of the Virgin Mary housed in the Jasna Gora monastery in Czestochowa, near the prison of Jacob Frank.

blood libel   The fabricated anti-Semitic allegation that Jews periodically killed Christian children to use their blood for rituals such as baking Passover matzoh. The blood libel was a common pretext for Jewish persecution and pogroms in the Middle Ages, but there have also been well-known cases in modern times, including the Damascus Affair (1840) and the Beilis Case (1911).

chuppa   Traditional Jewish wedding canopy held over the bride and groom during their wedding ceremony.

Conversos	Descendants of Spanish Jews who had converted to Christianity ("New Christians") during the times of the persecutions of the pogroms and Inquisition in the late fourteenth and fifteenth centuries. The parallel term for Portuguese Jews is Marrano.
David	Second (technically third) King of Israel (r. c.1010–970 BCE). His story is told primarily in Samuel I and II. A basic messianic doctrine of the Bible holds that the Messiah will be a male descendent of David.
Dhimmi	Protected people under the Muslim doctrine that "People of the Book" (Christians and Jews) could live in Muslim nations in peace and safety, and exercise their own religions (subject to certain restrictions on proselytizing, building new synagogues, etc.), provided they paid taxes and were loyal citizens.
Diaspora	Commonly used to describe the condition of dispersion (scattering) of the Jewish people living outside the Jewish homeland. Technically, the term "galut" (exile) refers to the condition of forced expulsion, while Diaspora refers to Jews' voluntary settlement outside of the homeland. All Jews today living outside the modern State of Israel are living in the Diaspora.
Donmeh	The secret sect of crypto-Jewish followers of Shabbatai Zevi who lived as Muslims in Salonika for three centuries.
disputation	A public debate between representatives of different religions over which is the true religion. The Inquisition used forced or sham disputations as an instrument of oppression against the Jews. The conversion to Judaism of the kingdom of Khazaria is commonly attributed to a genuine disputation won by the Jews in the eighth century.
Ethiopian Jewry (Beta Israel)	The Beta Israel is an Ethiopian ethnic group that observed a form of biblical Judaism. In the sixteenth century, they were thought to be part of the Ten Lost Tribes. At the end of the twentieth century, most of the

remaining Beta Israel (about 45,000) emigrated from Ethiopia to the State of Israel, about one-half through the "Operation Moses" and "Operation Solomon" airlifts.

Gaon   Originally the head of the Jewish academy in Babylonia. Later used as title for the heads of academies in Palestine, Egypt, Syria and other lands.

Gavirah   "The Lady"—Jacob Frank's title for his daughter Eva as the third member of the Frankist trinity of God, the Messiah (Frank), and the Lady.

gematria   The Hebrew language has no separate numerals, so each letter of the alphabet has a number value (*aleph* = 1; *bet* = 2; etc.). Gematria is a system of interpreting words according to the numerical value of their letters, often by substituting words having equivalent numerical value.

Geniza   Jewish law prohibits effacing or destroying the name of God. A Geniza was a burial place or storage chamber for unusable religious books and other writings that contained the name of God. The Cairo Geniza is a Jewish archeological treasure house; hundreds of thousands of pages of ancient works have been discovered there.

Hasid;   In general, pious Jews who follow a particular
Hasidim (pl.) religious ritual observance. Also used to describe the members of the seventeenth century Society of the Pious named after co-founder Judah Hasid, as well as (since the eighteenth century) the followers of modern Hasidism.

Hasidism   The popular Jewish movement, begun in the eighteenth century by the Ba'al Shem Tov, marked by an anti-intellectual emphasis on closeness to God through individual and communal joy. Individual groups of disciples (hasidim) followed a particular charismatic Master (tzadik, or rebbe).

Joseph, House of	A version of the Jewish messianic myth states that there will be two Messiahs. The first to appear will be a descendent of Joseph (through his son, Ephraim) who will be killed in battle but later resurrected when the second Messiah, a descendent of David, finally appears and establishes the messianic era of peace on earth.
Judaising	The practicing of Jewish religious customs by Christians (typically Conversos or Marranos), punishable by death under the Inquisition. Technically the Inquisition had jurisdiction only over actions by persons born or converted to Christianity (except for direct jurisdiction over Jews who committed open heresy or similar speech).
Kashrut	The system of rules defining ritual purity of foods, determining which foods and combinations of foods are kosher.
Khazaria	The nation on the Black Sea that converted to Judaism c.740 after a disputation among Jewish, Christian and Muslim representatives. The nation and its people essentially disappeared after the tenth century.
Ladino	Judeo-Spanish, a Hispanic language of Jews of Spanish origin.
Lost Tribes	The ten northern tribes of ancient Israel who disappeared after being conquered and scattered into captivity by the Assyrians in 722 BCE
Ma'aminim	The Believers—followers of Shabbatai Zevi.
ma'aser	Tithes demanded by Shukr Kuhayl II.
maggid	Lit., an instructor. Sometimes used for a preacher, but in Kabbalah the term refers to a heavenly spirit who appears and teaches esoteric knowledge to a Kabbalist. Joseph Karo used this name for the spirit who spoke to and through him.
Marrano	"New Christian" families of former Portuguese Jews

	who had converted, often under fear or force of the Inquisition. See Converso.
matzoh	Unleavened bread, eaten during the holiday of Passover to commemorate the Exodus of the Jews from Egypt under Moses.
menorah	A Jewish ritual candelabra. The Temple menorah described in Exodus 37:17-29 had seven lamps. The Chanukah menorah used today in homes for that holiday has eight candles, plus an extra one for the "helper" candle (shamas) used to light the others.
mezuzah	A small container holding a scroll with three biblical passages, placed on the doorways of Jewish homes.
mikvah	A ritual bath used to attain a state of spiritual purity, especially after menstrual cycle, upon conversion, or prior to the Sabbath and holidays.
mitzvah; *mitzvot (pl.)*	A biblical or religious commandment; sometimes used to describe any act of goodness.
Moshiach	Messiah; lit., "anointed one."
Podolia	The former name for the area of southern Poland in Ukraine.
rebbe	Hasidic term for rabbi.
responsa	Correspondence in which a recognized rabbinic authority answers a question concerning interpretation or application of ritual law.
Sambatyon *River*	The mythical river believed to separate the Ten Lost Tribes from the rest of the world. Stories placed it in Africa, Arabia, or India, and had it impassible on six days of the week (with the Jews forbidden to travel across it on the seventh day, the Sabbath).
seder	The ritual dinner and ceremony celebrating the Jewish holiday of Passover (the Jews' escape from captivity in Egypt).

Sephardi	Referring to the Jews originally settling in Spain and Portugal. See *Ashkenazi*.
Shabbat	The Sabbath; Saturday (the seventh day of the week in the Jewish calendar).
shatnes	The ritually prohibited mixture of two species, such as seeds, or fibers in cloth. (Deut. 22:9-11; Lev. 19:19.)
Shekhinah	A Kabbalistic concept of the spirit of God, generally as a feminine aspect.
shofar	A ram's horn, blown as a signal or warning sound, or used in religious ceremonies. According to Jewish legend, the appearance of the Messiah will be heralded by the sound of the shofar. (Isaiah 27:13)
Shulhan Auruch	A book detailing the rules of Jewish practice, written by Rabbi Joseph Karo (1565).
talit; talesim (pl.)	The fringed prayer shawl traditionally worn by men during daytime prayer services.
talit katan	The rectangular garment with four fringes, which is worn throughout the day by observant Jewish men.
tikun	The Kabbalistic concept of working to repair the imperfect world. Isaac Luria declared that efforts of tikun were an important individual obligation that could bring on the messianic era.
Torah	The Hebrew Bible. The term (meaning "instruction" or "teaching") has different technical meanings in different contexts, and can refer to the Pentateuch (the Five Books of Moses), to the complete Hebrew Bible (the Pentateuch, the Prophets, and the Writings), or to the complete Hebrew Bible together with the "Oral Law" also transmitted to Moses and explicated in the Talmud.
tzadik	Lit., "man of righteousness"—a Hasidic master.
yeshivah; yeshivot (pl.)	An academy of Jewish study.

Yigdal   A traditional Jewish prayer based upon Maimonides's
                    Thirteen Principles of Judaism.

Zohar   The basic book of the Kabbalah, written (or compiled)
                    by Sephardi Jews in the thirteenth century, but ascribed
                    to the sayings of Rabbi Shimon bar Yohai in Palestine.

SOURCES AND BIBLIOGRAPHY

No WORK on Jewish messianism can fail to acknowledge the extraordinary contribution and influence of Gershom Scholem. It is rare when an entire subject area of knowledge depends upon the enthusiasm, scholarship, and writings of a single scholar. Gershom Scholem was not satisfied to leave the history and analysis of Jewish messianism, and especially the phenomenon of Shabbatai Zevi, relegated to the embarrassed footnotes of Jewish history. His monumental work, *Sabbatai Sevi: The Mystical Messiah, 1626–1676,* together with the classic collection of his essays published as *The Messianic Idea in Judaism* as well as his articles for the *Encyclopedia Judaica,* would have been sufficient by themselves to reform modern Jewish thinking about messianism. In addition, these writings have been responsible for inspiring many other authors' works that now comprise the body of contemporary scholarship on the topic.

Besides Gershom Scholem's writings, three other sources have been especially helpful in collecting the stories of the Jewish Messiahs. The *Encyclopedia Judaica CD ROM Edition* is a wonderfully rich and convenient format unlocking a wealth of Jewish scholarship. The recent publication of Harold Lenowitz's *The Jewish Messiahs* while I was writing this book was a definite boon to me. Mr. Lenowitz's fine book provides translations of many key sources for the Messiah stories, as well as broad coverage and valuable analysis of the causes and connections of messianic movements. Another very helpful source was the collection of studies by leading scholars published as *Essential Papers on Messianic Movements and Personalities in Jewish History,* edited by Marc Saperstein. It was a great convenience to have access to the work of so many historians who write with such authority about specific aspects of Jewish messianism.

The above four works have provided invaluable information for retelling the stories that appear in this book. This book has also been based upon many other helpful works included in the following selected bibliography of principal sources consulted:

ASCHERSON, NEAL. (1995). *Black Sea.* New York: Hill and Wang.
American Psychiatric Association. Diagnostic and Statistical Manual of Mental Disorders (1994). 4th ed. Washington, D.C.
BAER, YITZHAK. (1961). *A History of the Jews in Christian Spain.* Philadelphia: Jewish Publication Society.
BEN ISRAEL, MENASSEH [Manassah]. (1650; reprint, 1987). *The Hope of Israel.* Trans. Moses Wall [second, corrected version of 1652]. Ed. Henry Méchoulan and Gérard Nahon. Oxford: Oxford University Press.
BIALIK, HAYIM NAHMAN, and YEHOSHUA HARA RAVNITZKY, eds. (1995). *The Book of Legends (Sefer Ha-Aggadah)* [CD-ROM version]. Trans. William G. Braude. Chicago: Davka Corporation.
BLADY, KEN. (2000). *Jewish Communities in Exotic Places.* Northvale, NJ: Jason Aronson.
BOTEACH, SHMUEL. (1993). *The Wolf Shall Lie with the Lamb— The Messiah in Hasidic Thought.* Northvale, NJ: Jason Aronson.
CHARLESWORTH, J. H., ed. (1992). *The Messiah: Developments in Earliest Judaism and Christianity.* Minneapolis: Fortess Press.
CHAYAT, SHLOMIT, SARA ISRAELI, and HILLA KOBLINER. (1990). *Hebrew from Scratch.* Jerusalem: Academon.
DIMONT, MAX I. (1962). *Jews, God and History.* New York: Signet.
DURANT, WILL. (1950). *The Age of Faith.* New York: Simon and Schuster.
FRANKEL, JONATHAN. (1997). *The Damascus Affair: "Ritual Murder,"* Politics, and the Jews in 1840. New York: Cambridge University Press.
FREEDMAN, H., trans. (1983). *Midrash Rabbah, Genesis.* New York: Soncino Press.

FREUD, SIGMUND. (1960). *Jokes and their Relation to the Unconscious.* Trans. James Strachey. New York: W. W. Norton.

GARBER, HELEN. (Spring 2000). Sergent Ephraim Selamolela. *Lifestyles 5760 Magazine,* 28:167, 43-46.

GILBERT, MARTIN. (1992). *The Atlas of Jewish History.* New York: Wm. Morrow.

GREENSTONE, JULIUS H. (1906). *The Messiah Idea in Jewish History.* Philadelphia: Jewish Publication Society of America.

HALEVI, JEHUDA. "KUZARI," ([1506]; reprint, abridged, 1969). Ed. Isaak Heinemann, In *Three Jewish Philosophers.* New York: Atheneum.

HALKIN, ABRAHAM [trans.] and DAVID HARTMAN. (1985). *Crisis and Leadership: Epistles of Maimonides.* Philadelphia: Jewish Publication Society of America.

HERTZBERG, ARTHUR. (Summer 1999). *Storming heaven—the perils of Jewish messianism.* Reform Judaism Magazine, 10.

IDEL, MOSHE. (1998). *Messianic Mystics.* New Haven: Yale University Press.

JACOBOVICI, SIMCHA. (1998). A lost tribe ignored by Jerusalem. *Boston Globe* [website archives at www.boston.com/globe], 17 August.

JOINT COMMITTEE ON THE NEW TRANSLATION OF THE BIBLE. (1961; reprint, 1972). *The New English Bible.* New York: Oxford University Press.

JOLKOVSKY, BINYAMIN L. (1998). The "Messiah Wars" heat up; online gets out of line. *The Jewish World Review* [online edition at www.jewishworldreview.com/0298/deutch1.html], 19 February.

JOSEPHUS [, FLAVIUS]. (1736; reprint, 1988). *The Works of Josephus.* Trans. William Whiston. N.p.: Henrickson Publishers.

KASTEIN, JOSEPH. (1931). *The Messiah of Ismir.* New York: Viking Press.

KLAUSNER, J. (1955). *The Messianic Idea in Israel.* New York: Macmillan.

LENOWITZ, HARRIS. (1998). *The Jewish Messiahs.* New York: Oxford University Press.

LEVIN, MEYER. (1931; reprint, 1985). *Classic Hassidic Tales.* New York: Dorset Press.

MANDEL, D., trans. (1995). *The CD ROM Bible* [part of the CD ROM Judaic Classics Library]. Chicago: Davka.

MARKS, RICHARD G. (1994). *The Image of Bar Kokhba in Traditional Jewish Literature.* University Park, PA: Pennsylvania State University Press.

MCFARLING, USHA LEE. (2000). One giant leap for machinekind? *Los Angeles Times,* 31 August, p.1.

NEUSNER, JACOB, WILLIAM SCOTT GREEN, and ERNEST S. FRERICHS, eds. (1987). *Judaisms and Their Messiahs.* New York: Cambridge University Press.

NEUSNER, JACOB, trans. (1987). *The Talmud of the Land of Israel [The Jerusalem Talmud].* Chicago: University of Chicago Press.

PARISE, FRANK, ed. (1982). *The Book of Calendars.* New York: Facts on File.

PATAI, RAPHAEL. (1979). *The Messiah Texts.* New York: Avon Books.

PEPYS, SAMUEL. (1983). *Diary.* Ed. Robert Latham and William Matthews. Berkeley: University of California Press.

PICARD, LIZA. (1998). *Restoration London.* New York: St. Martin's Press.

PLINY [the Elder]. (1963). *Natural History.* Trans. W.H.S. Jones. Cambridge: Harvard University Press.

RABBINICAL ASSEMBLY OF AMERICA-UNITED SYNAGOGUE OF AMERICA. (1946; reprint, 1973). *Sabbath and Festival Prayer Book.* Np.

REZNICK, LEIBEL. (1996). *The Mystery of Bar Kokhba.* Northvale, NJ: Jason Aronson.

SADEK, VLADIMIR. (1984). Solomon Molcho (c. 1500-1532) and his teachings. *Judaica Bohemiae* [State Jewish Museum, Prague] 20:2, pp. 84-96.

SALDARINI, ANTHONY J., trans. (1975). *The Fathers According to Rabbi Nathan (Abot de Rabbi Nathan)* Version B. Leiden: E.J.Brill.

SAPERSTEIN, MARC, ed. (1992). *Essential Papers on Messianic Movements and Personalities in Jewish History.* New York: New York University Press.

SCHIFFMAN, LAWRENCE H. (1998). *Texts and Traditions: A Source Reader for the Study of Second Temple and Rabbinic Judaism.* Hoboken, NJ: KTAV Publishing House.

SCHLEIFER, YIGAL and GERSHOM GORENBERG. (21 June 1999). Chabad's Messiah complex. *The Jerusalem Report Magazine,* 30-34.

SCHOLEM, GERSHOM. (1963). The Sprouting of the Horn of the Son of David—A New Source from the Beginnings of the Doenme Sect in Salonika," In I*n the Time Of Harvest—Essays in Honor of Abba Hillel Silver.* Ed. Daniel Jeremy Silver. New York: Macmillan.

———. (1971). *The Messianic Idea in Judaism.* New York: Schocken Books.

———. (1957; reprint, 1973) *Sabbatai Sevi: The Mystical Messiah,* 1626-1676. Princeton: Princeton University Press.

SCHRAM, PENINNAH. (1997). *Tales of Elijah the Prophet.* Northvale, NJ: Jason Aronson Inc.

SCHWARZ, LEO W. (1935). *The Jewish Caravan.* New York: Rinehart.

SHAROT, STEPHEN. (1982). *Messianism, Mysticism, and Magic.* Chapel Hill: University of North Carolina Press.

SHTULL-TRAURING, SIMCHA, ed. (1997). *Letters from Beyond the Sambatyon* [with accompanying CD-ROM]. New York: MAXIMA New Media.

SILVER, ABBA HILLEL. (1927; reprint, 1959) *A History of Messianic Speculation in Israel from the First through the Seventeenth Centuries.* Boston: Beacon Hill

The Soncino Talmud [CD version]. (1995). CD ROM Judaic Classics Library. Chicago: Davka.

SCHERMAN, RABBI NOSSON, ed. (1996). *The Tanach* [Stone Edition]. New York: Mesorah Publications.

TWERSKY, ISADORE, ed. (1972). *A Maimonides Reader.* New York: Behrman House.

URBACH, EPHRAIM E. (1969; reprint, 1975). *The Sages: Their Concepts and Beliefs. Trans. Israel Abrahams.* Jerusalem: Magnus Press, Hebrew University.

USQUE, SAMUEL. (1553; reprint, 1977). *Consolation for the Tribulations of Israel.* Trans. Martin A. Cohen. Philadelphia: Jewish Publication Society.

WADE, NICHOLAS. (1999). DNA backs a tribe's tradition of early descent from the Jews. *The New York Times,* 9 May, p. 1.

WIGODER, GEOFFREY, ed. *Encyclopedia Judaica* [CD-ROM Edition 1.0]. (1997). Jerusalem: Judaica Multimedia (Israel) Ltd.

WISE, MICHAEL O. (1999). *The First Jewish Messiah.* San Francisco: Harper San Francisco.

WOODWARD, KENNETH L. (1 November 1999). The way the world ends. *Newsweek,* pp. 66-74.

INDEX

A. The Messiahs (See also detailed entries in General Index)

B. General Index

A

Abarbanel, Isaac: calculations by, 58
Abdallah, Yusuf (Messiah), 146–47
Abner, Bishop of Burgos (Solomon Ha-Levi): as Converso, 160 n. 16, 161 n. 17
  Messiah stories, 160 n. 16
Abraham (son of Shabbatai Zevi) *See* Zevi, Shabbatai
Abu Isa (Messiah), 23–26
  ecumenical message, 25
  House of Joseph, 24
  Jesus as model, 24
  Lost Tribes, 25
  Maimonides recounts, 25, 33
  Mohammed as model, 24
  Sambatyon River, 25
  successors, 26–27
Abulafia, Abraham (Messiah), 46–49
  calculations, 48
  Kabbalah contributions, 47
  kills Nicholas II, 47–48, 150–160 n. 15
  Sambatyon River search, 47
  Solomon Adret opposes, 48
Abulafia, Samuel (Messiah), 50–52
  serves Don Pedro (King of Castile), 51–52
Abydos prison. *See* Zevi, Shabbatai
Adret, Solomon ben Abraham of Barcelona (the Rashba):
  opposes Abraham Abulafia, 48
  opposes Nissim ben Abraham, 49

Akiba, Rabbi: background, 157 n. 8
  opposed by Yochanan ben Torta, 13
  Sambatyon River belief, 163 n. 27
  support for Bar Kokhba, 12, 52
al-Dar'l, Moshe (Moses, Messiah), 34–35
  Maimonides retells, 34–35
  predictions of events, 35
al-Din, Zun (Turkish Sultan): arranges for death of David Alroy, 41
Aleander, Hieronymous: opposes David Reuveni, 68
al-Fayyumi, Jacob ben Nathanel: asks about the Yemenite Messiah, 32
Alroy, David (Messiah), 38–42
  Arabian Nights style, 38, 42
  Baghdad fraud follows, 44
  Benjamin Disraeli recounts, 42
  Benjamin of Tudela recounts, 42
  decapitation by father-in-law, 41
  escapes from prison, 40
  father as Elijah, 39
  floats across Gozan River on kerchief, 40
  Khazaria relationship, 39
apocrypha: and Messiah, 2
Arabia: location of Lost Tribes, 163 n. 26
  origin claimed by David Reuveni, 64
Arabian Nights. See Alroy, David
Armilus, King: adversary of Messiah, 4
Ashkenazi: first Ashkenazi Messiah, 57
  Shabbatai Zevi, 92, 102

H

Hadrian (Emperor of Rome): attempts to pacify Jews, 9
  reconstruction of Temple, 9
  report to Senate, 10
Halevi, Yehudah: writes about Khazaria, 159 n. 14
Ha-Levi, Solomon. *See* Abner, Bishop of Burgos
Ha-Lorki, Joshua. *See* Heronimo de Santa Fe
Hasid, Judah: companion of Hayim Malakh, 117–18
Hasidim: Society of the Pious, 117–18
Hasidism: and Messiahs, 134–37
Hayim ben Shlomo. *See* Hayim Malakh
Hayim Malakh (Hayim ben Shlomo, Messiah), 117–18
Hayyun, Nehemiah Hiyya (Messiah), 118
Hebron: miracle by David Reuveni, 63
Henry VIII (King of England): Clement VII conflict, 172–73
Heronimo de Santa Fe (Joshua Ha-Lorki): as Converso, 161 n. 17
Herrera, Maid of. *See* Ines
Hillel, Rabbi: teachings to apply until messianic era, 12
Hisdai ibn Shaprut: Khazaria correspondence, 159 n. 14
Holocaust: as birth pangs, 152
horse: and David Reuveni, 60, 64
  and the Messiah, 161 n. 19, 162 n. 21

I

Ibn Ayre (Messiah), 33–34
  Maimonides recounts, 33–34
  not claiming to be Messiah, 34
  punishment by Jewish community, 34
India. *See* Sambatyon River
Ines, Maid of Herrera: women's role in Messiah history, 55
Inquisition: Dona Juana Enriquez tortured, 56
  Ines, Maid of Herrera, burned, 55
  limited jurisdiction over Jews, 162 n. 22
  Ludovico Diaz burned, 53
  Shlomo Molkho burned, 76
  Shlomo Molkho saved by Clement VII, 74–75
  suspended for David Reuveni, 67
Iran. *See* Persia
Isabella (Queen of Spain). *See* Ferdinand and Isabella
Isaiah: views of Messiah, 2
Isaphanites. *See* Isavites
Isavites: followers of Abu Isa, 26
Ishmael (son of Shabbatai Zevi). *See* Zevi, Shabbatai
Islam: and Abu Isa, 24
  control of Holy Land, 64
  Jewish messianism influenced by, 20–21, 24–25
  Jews as protected people, 33, 34
Ismir. *See* Smyrna
Israel: Jews return in twentieth century, 148
Israel of Ruzhin (Messiah), 137

M

General World and Jewish History	Century Beginning	50 Jewish Messiahs
Scattering of the Lost Tribes (722 BCE)	800	
Book of Deuteronomy found (622 BCE)	700	
Destruction of First Temple and Exile to Babylonia (586 BCE)	600	Zerubbabel (519)
The Persian Wars (490–479 BCE) Age of Pericles, Athens (450–430 BCE)	500	
Aristotle (384–322 BCE) Alexander the Great (r. 336–323 BCE)	400	
The Punic Wars between Rome and Carthage (264-146 BCE)	300	
Judah Maccabee (164 BCE)	200	
Caesar invades Britain (55 BCE) Roman Empire founded (27 BCE)	100	"Judah," Teacher of Righteousness (1st Cent. BCE)
Jesus Christ (4 BCE?–29 CE?) Revolt of the Zealots (Simon ben Gioras, John ben Levy, Eleazar ben Simon, and Menahem ben Judas) Second Temple Destroyed (70 CE) Fall of Masada (73 CE)	CE	Theudas (44 CE)
Fall of Betar (135 CE)	100	Simeon Bar Kokhba (c. 100–135 CE)
Diocletian saves Roman Empire (r. 284-306)	200	
Division of Roman Empire (395)	300	
Goths sack Rome (410)	400	Moses of Crete (440)
Franks conquer France, Belgium, and other parts of Europe	500	
Mohammed's Hegira (622)	600	The Syrian Messiah (643)
Muslim invasion of Iberia (711) Khazaria converts to Judaism (740)	700	Serenus (720) Abu Isa (750)
Charlemagne crowned Emperor (800)	800	Yudghan of Hamadan (800) Mushka (9th c.)
Magyar invasion of Europe defeated by Otto the Great (955)	900	
First Crusade (1096)	1000	The Lyons Messiah (1060)
Elijah appears to the Caliph of Baghdad (1120) Moses Maimonides (1135–1204) "The Year of Flying" (1147)	1100	Ibn Ayre (1100) Moshe al-Dar'l (1120) David Alroy (active 1120–1147) The Yemenite Messiah (1192)
King John signs Magna Carta (1215) Pope Nicholas II dies (1280)	1200	Abraham Abulafia (1240–1291) Nissim ben Abraham, Prophet of Avila (1295)